D1571574

THEY NEVER SURRENDERED

THE LAKOTA SIOUX BAND
THAT STAYED IN CANADA

4th Edition Revised

THEY NEVER SURRENDERED

THE LAKOTA SIOUX BAND
THAT STAYED IN CANADA

RONALD J. PAPANDREA

4th Edition Revised
Printed on acid-free paper
Published by Lightning Source
An INGRAM Company
La Vergne, Tennessee, USA
Kiln Farm, Milton Keynes, UK

LCCN: 2007904506

Paperback ISBN: 978-0-9746527-8-8

Paperback Retail Price: $19.99 USD, £14.99 GBP, €17.99 EUR

Hardcover Retail Price: $29.99 USD, £19.99 GBP, €24.99 EUR

Hardcover ISBN: 978-0-9746527-7-1

**Available from all major English language book distributors
with 55% wholesale discount and returns accepted.**

This book is dedicated to Kathie:

by the Gaspe Bay
the snow swirling as it falls
at your fire warm

près de la Baie de Gaspé
la neige tournoyant dans sa chute
à la chaleur de ton feu

The Sixth Grandfather

… Four more riders, one from each quarter,
Came forth and presented me with a hoop,
And with that hoop I was to make a nation
And under that we were to prosper …

I could hear many voices cheering.
The (six) grandfathers were sitting
With their arms and palms out
And said: "He has triumphed!"

The first grandfather said:
"Behold (this) cup;
In this cup your nation and you
Shall feed from it."

The second grandfather said:
"Now you shall go forth.
Your people are in great difficulty.
Behold them!"

The third grandfather said:
"On earth the beings
Will be glad to see you.
So take courage."

The fourth grandfather said:
"The road of the generations you shall walk.
Your grandfathers shall watch over you
In all the four quarters of the earth."

The fifth grandfather said:
"Every day (an) eagle shall be over you.
He has eyes that will see everything,
And through them you shall also see."

The sixth grandfather said:
"Behold them, with great difficulty they shall walk
And you shall go among them. Behold them,
This is your nation and you shall go back to them."

Black Elk (1863-1950)

From The Sixth Grandfather, edited by
Raymond J. DeMallie, pages 123-141.

CONTENTS

APPENDICES

INDEX

LIST OF ILLUSTRATIONS

SPECIAL THANKS TO:

Margaux Allard, Lakota Sioux Band Member, Wood Mountain, Saskatchewan
Calvin Bear First, Dakota Band Member, Fort Peck, Montana
Guy Birchard, Antiquarian Bookseller, Moose Jaw, Saskatchewan
Vicki Birkeland, Lakota Sioux Band Member, Cheyenne River, South Dakota
David Black Moon, Lakota Sioux Band Member, Cheyenne River, South Dakota
Gabe Black Moon, Lakota Sioux Band Member, Cheyenne River, South Dakota
Norma Black Moon, Lakota Sioux Band Member, Cheyenne River, SD
Norvan Black Moon, Lakota Sioux Band Member, Cheyenne River, SD
LaDonna Brave Bull Allard, Tribal Tourism, Standing Rock, North Dakota
Kingsley M. Bray, Historian, Manchester, England, United Kingdom
Bruce Brownwolf, Lakota Sioux Band Member, Cheyenne River, South Dakota
Ephriam D. Dickson III, Historian, Salt Lake City, Utah
Annie Donofrio, Historian, Littleton, Colorado
Andrew Ferguson, Lakota Sioux Band Member, Wood Mountain, Saskatchewan
Judy Fitzpatrick, Wood Mountain Post Provincial Park, Saskatchewan
Randy Gaudry, Métis Leader, Willow Bunch, Saskatchewan
Linda Kennedy Gaudry, Transcribed Légaré Depositions, Willow Bunch, SK
Ray Glasrud, Wild Prairie Rancher, Shaunavon, Saskatchewan
Lloyd Goodtrack, Lakota Sioux Singer and Drummer, Wood Mountain, SK
Alvina Hump, Lakota Sioux Band Member, Cheyenne River, South Dakota
Bev Johnson, Lakota Sioux Band Secretary, Wood Mountain, Saskatchewan
Gord Johnson, Moose Jaw Ambassador to the World, Moose Jaw, Saskatchewan
Leith Knight, Writer, Moose Jaw Times-Herald, Moose Jaw, Saskatchewan
Karen Lamb, Dakota Club Library, Eagle Butte, South Dakota
Ernie LaPointe, Lakota Historian, Lead, South Dakota
Sonja LaPointe, Lakota Historian, Lead, South Dakota
Bill LeCaine, Lakota Sioux Band Member and Former NHL Player
Ellen LeCaine, Lakota Sioux Band Councillor, Wood Mountain, Saskatchewan
Grace Peigan LeCaine, Lakota Sioux, Pasqua Reserve, Saskatchewan
Gus LeCaine, Lakota Sioux Band Member, Wood Mountain, Saskatchewan
John LeCaine, Lakota Sioux Band Member, Wood Mountain, Saskatchewan
Margaret Schmaltz LeCaine, Lakota Band Member, Wood Mountain, SK
Preston LeCaine, Lakota Sioux Band Member, Wood Mountain, Saskatchewan
Leonard Lethbridge Sr., Lakota Sioux Band Member, Wood Mountain, SK
Loretta Lethbridge, Lakota Sioux Band Councillor, Wood Mountain, SK
Ross Lethbridge, Lakota Sioux Band Member, Wood Mountain, Saskatchewan
Mary C. Marino, Ph.D., Professor, University of Saskatchewan
Elizabeth Michalski, Lakota Sioux Band Member, Moose Jaw, Saskatchewan
Jim Nelson, Timber Lake Topic, Timber Lake, South Dakota
Bill Ogle, Lakota Sioux Band Member, Wood Mountain, Saskatchewan
Crystal Ogle, Wood Mountain, Saskatchewan
David Ogle, Lakota Sioux Band Councillor, Wood Mountain, Saskatchewan
Travis Ogle, Lakota Sioux Band Chief, Wood Mountain, Saskatchewan
Todd Peigan, Lakota Sioux, Pasqua Reserve, Saskatchewan
Donna Rae Petersen, Cultural Programs Administrator, Cheyenne River, SD
Thelma Poirier, Poet and Historian, Wood Mountain, Saskatchewan
Alison Sherwin, Lakota Sioux Band Councillor, Wood Mountain, Saskatchewan
Barb Silvester, Moose Jaw Public Library, Moose Jaw, Saskatchewan
Bill Thompson, Lakota Sioux Band Member, Cheyenne River, Saskatchewan
Claire Thomson, Lakota Sioux University Student, Rockglen, Saskatchewan
Elizabeth Thomson, Historian, Rockglen, Saskatchewan
Harold Thomson, Lakota Sioux descendent, Rockglen, Saskatchewan
Rory Thomson, Historian, Rockglen, Saskatchewan
Joane Pappas White, Attorney and Rancher, Price, Utah
JD Williams, Lakota Sioux Band Member, Cheyenne River, South Dakota
Maurice Williams, Lakota Sioux Band Member, Cheyenne River, South Dakota
Mona Williams, Lakota Sioux Band Member, Cheyenne River, South Dakota
Ron Walter, Writer, Moose Jaw Times-Herald, Moose Jaw, Saskatchewan

"I left several families at Wood Mountain
and between there and Qu'Appelle."

Sitting Bull
July 20, 1881[1]

I. THEY NEVER SURRENDERED

SITTING BULL surrendered himself and 187 of his band at Fort Buford, Dakota Territory, on July 19, 1881. Their guns and horses were taken; but Sitting Bull was permitted to keep his Winchester rifle, which he gave up the next day during his surrender speech, and which allowed him to say "I wish it to be remembered that I was the last man of my tribe to surrender his rifle."[2] However, a Lakota Sioux band of over 200 people remained in Canada; they still had their guns and they still had their horses. The fate of this band, now known as the "Wood Mountain Lakota", is the subject of this book (Appendix A, Divisions of the Sioux Nation and Some of Their Chiefs).

During the four and one half years the Lakota Sioux were in Canada, the Canadian government steadfastly maintained a policy of tolerating them as refugees, but refused to grant them a reserve or other assistance. The Canadian government, pressured by the Americans and having a much smaller national budget, wanted the Lakota Sioux to return to the United States and settle on reservations there. This official policy was sometimes softened by the actions of Canadians in close contact with the Lakota Sioux, such as James Morrow Walsh of the North-West Mounted Police (NWMP) and Jean Louis Légaré, a French-Canadian who traded with the Indians. At this point, it is helpful to be aware of ten basic facts about the Canadian plains during the years 1867-1885:

1. Canada became a nation July 1, 1867, made up of four provinces: Ontario, Quebec, New Brunswick and Nova Scotia.
2. The Hudson's Bay Company (HBC) sold its land, including the Canadian plains, to Canada in 1869.

1

3. The Canadian plains are bordered on the east by the Red River (which is also the Minnesota-North Dakota border) and on the west by the Canadian Rocky Mountains. To the north it extends roughly along a line connecting the cities of Winnipeg (the east end of the plains, 60 miles north of the U.S. border), Saskatoon (the middle of the plains, 240 miles north of the U.S. border), and Edmonton (the west end of the plains, 340 miles north of the U.S. border). This area is contained within the Provinces of Manitoba, Saskatchewan and Alberta; and sustains a greater population than the northern U.S plains (Appendix B, Overview Map).

4. The American-Canadian border across the plains was first surveyed and marked during 1873 and 1874. These same years, Canada formed the North-West Mounted Police (NWMP) with an authorized strength of 300 men. Its initial purpose was to enforce Canadian law and sovereignty within the Canadian plains, west of the Province of Manitoba.

5. During 1871-1877, the Canadian government made treaties with the "Canadian" Indian tribes that were on the Canadian plains. These Indians were allowed reserves and were given treaty benefits, but they gave up their rights to vast areas of the Canadian plains.

6. During 1874-1881, the Canadian government granted reserves to some Dakota Sioux bands in Canada, including the bands of Chief Standing Buffalo (the son) and Chief White Cap. These were "American" Indians who went to Canada as a result of the Dakota Sioux War of 1862, in Minnesota. They were given Canadian reserves but they were not entitled to treaty benefits or other assistance (they were "non-treaty" Indians).

7. By 1881, the Americans had largely succeeded in eliminating the buffalo and free roaming plains Indians faced starvation; as well as the Métis (people who were part Indian, who usually spoke at least one Indian language and who conducted organized buffalo hunts).

8. The Canadian Pacific Railway, advancing from Winnipeg (the east end of the plains), reached Regina and Moose Jaw (the middle of the plains) in 1882; it reached Calgary (the west end of the plains) in 1883. The railway linked up with the Pacific coast of Canada in 1885.

9. The Métis, Led by Louis Riel, fought two wars of resistance against the Canadian government. The Resistance of 1869-70 resulted in the creation of the Province of Manitoba, but Riel was forced to go into exile in the United States. The Resistance of 1885 was defeated at the Battle of Batoche. In the 1885 resistance the Métis had some Indian allies, including some Lakota Sioux.

10. During 1876-1878, as a result of the Sioux War if 1876, thousands of Lakota Sioux went to the Wood Mountain area of Canada, where there was a small Métis community and where some Dakota Sioux liked to camp. Wood Mountain is a hilly area that had water, wood and game, including buffalo; and it was a place where Canadians traded with Indians. The Lakota Sioux needed to trade, especially for ammunition.

II. WOOD MOUNTAIN

AFTER the Battle of the Little Big Horn, June 25-26, 1876, the U.S. army continued to pursue free roaming Indians. In the fall some Chiefs decided to go to Canada to escape the army. On December 18, 1876, 57 Lakota Sioux lodges were in Canada at Wood Mountain, near the trading post of Jean Louis Légaré. On December 19, 1876, Black Moon, the Hunkpapa Chief, arrived with 52 lodges. The NWMP counted 2,900 Lakota Sioux at Wood Mountain, including a large proportion of women and children.[3] On March 3, 1877, Four Horns, the Hunkpapa Chief who was the brother of Sitting Bull's father, crossed into Canada with 57 lodges.[4] By early April, 1877, the NWMP had three men stationed at a small "lookout" post in Wood Mountain[5] (Appendix C, Detail Map).

Sitting Bull, Crazy Horse, and other Chiefs, met during the last two weeks of January, 1877; north of where Sheridan, Wyoming, is now located.[6] The Chiefs debated between war or surrender in the U.S.; or escape to Canada. Crazy Horse led his people to Camp Robinson, Nebraska, and surrendered on May 6, 1877. About that time, Sitting Bull was crossing the "Medicine Line" and entered Canada with 135 lodges.[7]

After Crazy Horse was killed at Camp Robinson, September 5, 1877, more bands of Lakota Sioux went to Canada. There are many stories about the dying words of Crazy Horse. In one story he is quoted: "I have always wanted to go to the land of the Grandmother (Canada). I shall be dead in a few minutes and will then go to the Grandmother's country. I want you all to follow me."[8] Ten weeks later, his followers were among two columns being moved to new agencies. Indian Agent Irwin stated: "When about 75 miles en route, over 2,000 northern Indians broke away from the Spotted Tail column … and made a descent upon us, and threatened to involve us in serious difficulty … by causing a general outbreak. They brought with them the remains of Crazy Horse in order to madden our Indians, but in this they failed, and the major portion finally struck off north."[9]

By the spring of 1878, the number of Lakota Sioux in Canada peaked at around 5,000.[10] However, the killing of the buffalo was depleting the food supply of all free roaming plains Indians and also the Métis. During 1878-1881, the vast majority of Lakota Sioux in Canada returned to the United States and settled on reservations.

The winter of 1880-81 was hard for Sitting Bull. His people were starving and many Chiefs decided to surrender. Black Moon, Gall and Crow surrendered 305 people to the U.S. on January 2, 1881, and they were marched to Fort Buford, Dakota Territory.[11] On January 29, 1881, Iron Dog surrendered 64 people and they were also taken to Fort Buford.[12] Crow King surrendered 350 people at Fort Buford on February 5, 1881.[13] Low Dog surrendered 135 people at Fort Buford on April 11, 1881.[14]

III. WILLOW BUNCH

THE main focus of this book is on the Lakota Sioux Band, and its subgroups, that stayed in Canada after Sitting Bull returned to the United States. Sitting Bull surrendered 188 people from 35 families[15]: 188/35 = 5.4 per family. For the year 1881, I use 5.4 as the average family size, to calculate population figures when a source refers to a number of Lakota Sioux "families" or "lodges".

On April 20, 1881, Sitting Bull was camped thirty-eight miles east of the Wood Mountain NWMP Post, in the Métis community of Willow Bunch; near the trading post of Jean Louis Légaré.[16] In 1880 Légaré had moved his store from Wood Mountain.[17] Légaré gave the Lakota Sioux a feast, but advised them to return to the United States. Légaré stated there were 485 Lakota Sioux at the feast.[18] This figure could have been a little inflated because Légaré was seeking reimbursement from the American government. (Appendix D, The "485" Figure in the Légaré Bill).

After the feast, sixteen families (about 86 people) left Sitting Bull and went 200 miles northwest to Moose Woods; where there was a Dakota Sioux reserve.[19] This was the reserve selected by Chief White Cap in 1879 (Reserve #94 – White Cap) and is today about sixteen miles south of Saskatoon. A small Métis community, Round Prairie, was just south of the reserve, but no longer exists. On April 26, 1881, despite Sitting Bull's opposition, Légaré took 16 people to Fort Buford; but four of these were witnesses who returned to report on how their people were treated.[20] Sitting Bull's band was down to no more than 387 people.

IV. FORT QU'APPELLE

SITTING BULL made a last effort to obtain a reserve in Canada. He took most of his people 150 miles northeast to Ft. Qu'Appelle, where his friend, Superintendent Walsh (NWMP), had been transferred. Walsh was on sick leave back east. Sitting Bull met instead with the Indian Commissioner, Edgar Dewdney, who denied his request for a reserve.

Near the Légaré store, Sitting Bull had left about 80 or 90 people, including the four witnesses who would shortly return from Fort Buford. Most of these people were women, children and elders. While Sitting Bull was gone, Légaré took a second group to Fort Buford, this time 32 people; but three of these were witnesses who returned.[21] Among those who surrendered was the eldest daughter of Sitting Bull, who was eloping with her suitor; a grievous loss for her father.[22] The number of people near the Légaré store was down to around 50 or 60, including the three witnesses who returned from the second trip to Fort Buford.[23]

Sitting Bull failed in his attempt to get a Canadian reserve but some of his people decided to stay in the Fort Qu'Appelle area. Probably, a number of them found work in the Métis community of Lebret, which is nearby to the east. Probably, a number of the Lakota Sioux joined the Dakota Sioux at their reserve northwest of Fort Qu'Appelle. This was the reserve selected by Chief Standing Buffalo (the son) in 1877 (Reserve #78 – Standing Buffalo).

V. SITTING BULL RETURNS TO THE UNITED STATES

ON July 2, 1881, Sitting Bull reunited with those remaining near the Légaré store in Willow Bunch. Légaré, once again, gave the Lakota Sioux a feast. The total size of their camp was down to 300 people. On July 11, 1881, Légaré took 188 Lakota Sioux, including Sitting Bull, to Fort Buford; but one of these was a witness who returned to Willow Bunch.[24]

On the 150 mile trip to Fort Buford, seven Métis aided Légaré as interpreters, scouts and teamsters. Their names were: Narcisse Lecerte, Jean "Johnny" Chartrand, André Gaudry, Charles Champagne, Ambroise Delorme, Antoine Gosselin and Louison Piché. Lecerte was next in charge after Légaré and chief interpreter.[25] Chartrand and Gaudry also spoke Sioux. Referring to Sitting Bull, André Gaudry always said "It was a sad day to take my friend back to the United States but it had to be done."[26]

Remaining in Canada, we can estimate 113 Lakota Sioux at Willow Bunch, including the witness who returned with Légaré; 86 near Moose Woods and some near Fort Qu'Appelle. They probably represented all seven Lakota Sioux campfires: Hunkpapa, Mnicoujou, Oglala, Brulé, Sans Arc, Two Kettle and Blackfoot.[27] There were also some Lakota families living near the Wood Mountain NWMP Post.[28] These were the wives and children of some of the men at the post; or of Métis or traders. All together, over 200 Lakota remained in Canada after Sitting Bull left.

The Lakota Sioux who stayed behind at Willow Bunch watched Sitting Bull leave with a sinking feeling in their hearts. How would they survive without their greatest leader? The Canadian government was not going to give them a reserve. The buffalo were gone and small game was hunted out. However, their numbers were small so they needed less to sustain themselves. They had Dakota Sioux friends who had obtained reserves in Canada; and, they had Métis friends who also had to find a new way of life because they had been dependent on the buffalo too.

Prudent Lapointe came to Willow Bunch in August, 1883, two years after Sitting Bull left. He wrote: "… I was the fifth French Canadian to live in Willow Bunch which was comprised of some forty families, partly made up of Sioux Indians … The buffalo hunt having been poor the previous year, they had nothing to do except hunt game: muskrat, fox, prairie wolf, coyote … The older Métis found life hard because of the lack of buffalo meat and in the following years these same Métis who had lived off this good buffalo meat were reduced to gathering buffalo bones and selling them in Moose Jaw, eighty-five miles away, for $6.00 a ton … The winter of 1884 passed uneventfully except that I attended my first Sioux Indian Dance … Several families had wintered at Willow Bunch, the others having gone to Wood Mountain or Moose Jaw … We had a big store built of logs. One day, several chiefs asked Mr. Légaré permission to hold a dance. Having been granted permission, the chiefs … No Neck and Black Moon (the Mnicoujou Chief, not the Hunkpapa Chief with the same name) brought their people … The men wore loin cloths and a buffalo pelt to keep them warm in the winter, the women wore brightly colored dresses, blue, white, red, dappled with vermilion. Their orchestra consisted only of a big drum and four or six others. They were the first musicians that I heard in the West and I was so moved I wanted to cry …"[29] No Neck returned to the U.S and surrendered at Standing Rock agency, Dakota Territory, in May of 1884. He died prior to the 1885 census.[30]

VI. MOOSE JAW

In 1882, a boom-town began to develop at "The Turn" in the Moose Jaw River, 85 miles north of Willow Bunch. Previously, Moose Jaw had been a crossing point on the river and a good camping place for Indians and Métis; now, the Canadian Pacific Railway (CPR) was coming through from the east. Moose Jaw was at the right spot for a railway refueling station; it also had plenty of water for steam engines and settlers.

The first settlers in Moose Jaw lived and worked in tents, but they soon built houses and commercial buildings. On September 6, 1882, the first CPR work train arrived. On April 1, 1883, the first regularly scheduled passenger train arrived.[31] The first edition of the *Moose Jaw News*, May 4, 1883, stated "… everything required for a pioneer life is obtainable in Moose Jaw at reasonable prices …" The paper of January 18, 1884, stated that Moose Jaw had a population of 720. On January 19, 1884, Edgar Dewdney, who was now Lieutenant-Governor (Governor in the U.S.) of the North-West Territories, as well as the Indian Commissioner, signed a proclamation incorporating Moose Jaw as a town.[32]

In 1883, about 80 Lakota Sioux, moved to Moose Jaw and set up a continuous camp.[33] They were under the leadership of Black Bull. In 1878, James Walsh, NWMP, considered Black Bull to be among the important Lakota chiefs in Canada.[34] Black Bull was a Brulé Lakota. E.H. Allison was married to a Brulé Lakota and he spoke the Lakota Dialect. Allison wrote that Black Bull was a "chief noted for bravery." Black Bull fought at the Battle of the Little Big Horn and was wounded in the leg. Because of this injury, he was also known as "Lame Brulé".[35] Not all the Lakota Sioux moved to Moose Jaw. No Neck and Black Moon (the Mnicoujou Chief, not the Hunkpapa Chief with the same name) were still at Willow Bunch during the winter of 1883-84. The Lakota Sioux population at Moose Jaw varied because many still liked to roam and hunt.

John MacLean was a Methodist missionary. In 1896, he published a book with the unfortunate title *"Canadian Savage Folk"*. Despite the title, he made some good observations about the Lakota Sioux:

"Frequent visits made to the Sioux camp at Moose Jaw brought me into contact with these people, whom I found industrious even in their unsettled condition, the women working in the town at whatever they could find as washer-women, and the men splitting and sawing wood, or helping occasionally on the farms during harvest."

"Along the line of railroad a precarious livelihood is obtained by them, in polishing buffalo horns and making moccasins, which they sell to the traveling public. The children are happy in their poverty, scantily clad, yet full of joy when they are sporting in the water, or playing at spinning top."

"As the white traveler passes by their camp, the women and children seek their lodges, and peep through the holes at the stranger, and talk about him among themselves. Ask one of them his name, and he will turn to another of his friends to answer in his place. An aged chief was accustomed to spend much of his time around the stores, delighting to relate the story of his adventures and the exploits of his tribe. A genial old man was he, and yet, despite the familiarity of the two races, there was great fear manifested by some of the white people during the progress of the second Riel Rebellion (The Métis Resistance of 1885), lest they should join the rebels."

"The sad wails which I have heard in the Sioux camp when some little child has died has told more impressively than words could do, the depths and intensity of the mother's love. No hand is ever lifted to correct the children, and yet they are obedient to the instructions of their superiors."[36]

VII. THE MÉTIS RESISTANCE OF 1885

As previously mentioned, in the spring of 1881 sixteen Lakota Sioux families (about 86 people), left Sitting Bull's camp and went to Moose Woods, where a Dakota Sioux reserve was located (Reserve #94 – White Cap). Saskatoon was founded 16 miles north of that reserve. The Lakota Sioux worked for ranchers at Round Prairie, a small Métis community which formerly existed south of the reserve. In 1882, the band moved 60 miles northeast to Batoche, which was part of a Métis community much larger than Round Prairie. Again, the Lakota Sioux worked for Métis ranchers.[37] Gabriel Dumont, the military leader of the Métis, lived at Batoche and it became the center of the Métis Resistance of 1885.

In 1869, Louis Riel, a French Métis, led a revolt against the Canadian government. This resulted in the creation of the Province of Manitoba, but Riel was forced to go into exile in the United States. In 1885, joined by Gabriel Dumont as military leader, Riel led a second revolt. Of the four major battles of the Métis Resistance of 1885, three occurred in the Batoche area: The Battle of Duck Lake (March 26, 1885); The Battle of Fish Creek (April 20, 1885); and The Battle of Batoche (May 9-12, 1885).

The Battle of Duck Lake took place on a Cree Indian Reserve and the Métis were joined by a few Cree. Some Cree were also with the Métis at Fish Creek, along with some of Chief White Cap's band (Dakota Sioux), some Lakota Sioux and some Saulteaux (Ojibwa/Chippewa).[38] Indians from the same tribes were with the Métis at Batoche.

During first day of the Battle of Batoche the Métis were at their maximum strength. They had about 295-350 men, including 45-50 Indians. The Canadian government forces were led by Major General Frederick Middleton, a former British Officer with combat experience in New Zealand, India and Burma. Most of his 936 men were under-trained militia; but he also had four artillery pieces (9-pounders), a Gatling gun, and a great supply of ammunition; he received 50 additional men on the third day of the battle.[39] On the fourth day, the Métis lost when they ran out of ammunition and many of their men had quit the fight. The Battle of Batoche was decisive and the Métis Resistance of 1885 was soon over.

Some Lakota Sioux fought with the Métis in their Resistance of 1885. From the Lakota Sioux living near Batoche, Red Bear (Mato Luta); Teal Duck (Siyaka), with his brothers Tormenting Bear (Mato Wakakesija) and Poor Crow (Kangi Tomaheca); are known to have fought. Red Bear, Teal Duck and Poor Crow, were veterans of the Battle of the Little Big Horn, which took place in 1876.[40]

There are sources that place Black Bull, the chief at Moose Jaw, and He Killed Two (Big Joe Ferguson), with the Métis; and state that Black Bull was badly wounded.[41] However, I have to question those sources. Within eight weeks after Batoche, Canadian soldiers stationed at Moose Jaw took friendly pictures with Black Bull.[42] Also, a Canadian soldier at Moose Jaw wrote home that he met with Black Bull.[43] In addition, the Lakota Sioux at Moose Jaw provided scouts for the Canadian government. It is hard to believe, in a tribal society, band members living together would place themselves on opposite sides of a war.

A monument in the Batoche Cemetery lists four Métis killed at Duck Lake, Four at Fish Creek and eleven at Batoche. The monument lists a total of four Indian dead for all three engagements. Of the four Lakota Sioux known to have participated in the Métis Resistance of 1885, two died. Tormenting Bear was killed during the fighting. Red Bear died from his battle wound or from sickness, while serving his prison sentence.[44] (Appendix E, The Monument in the Batoche Cemetery and Appendix F, Photograph of Indian Names on the Batoche Monument).

In the Aftermath of the Métis Resistance, it was not a good idea to admit your participation. Louis Riel was tried and hung in Regina. The hanging is still intensely debated among French and English Canadians. In Battleford, eight Indians were put on trial for events outside the scope of this book. They were hung at the same time from the same platform.

In addition to Riel, eighteen Métis were tried in Regina and given prison sentences. Riel's secretary, a white man, was sent to a mental asylum. Forty-seven Indians served prison sentences of six months or more. Gabriel Dumont went into exile in the United States; as did others, including some Indians.[45] Only a small minority of Métis and Indians participated in the Métis Resistance of 1885 (Appendix G, The Trial of Two Lakota Sioux).

White Cap, the elderly Chief of the Dakota Sioux at Moose Woods (Reserve #94 – White Cap), became caught up in the Métis Resistance of 1885. He could not control his young men and some of them joined the resistance. The cattle on his reserve were taken by the Métis; and they escorted White Cap to Batoche. Riel made use of White Cap's reputation as a Dakota Sioux leader by putting him on the Métis governing council; but this was not something that White Cap sought, or even understood.

White Cap was put him on trial in Regina for treason-felony. Gerald Willoughby, a white trader and storekeeper living in Saskatoon, testified as to White Cap's good reputation and that White Cap was coerced into going to Batoche.[46] In somewhat of a miracle, a jury found the Chief "not guilty". White Cap gathered up his scattered band and brought them back to their reserve.[47] Chief White Cap died in 1889.[48]

During the Métis Resistance of 1885, some Lakota Sioux living at Batoche sent their women, children and elders to join the Lakota Sioux at Moose Jaw. Some of these people continued east to join the Lakota Sioux and the Dakota Sioux at Fort Qu'Appelle. After the fighting, most of the Lakota Sioux remaining in the Batoche area also went to Moose Jaw or to Fort Qu'Appelle.[49] Some Lakota Sioux may have joined White Cap at Moose Woods and some may have gone to Prince Albert, 35 miles northeast of Batoche.

Unlike the Lakota Sioux living near the Métis at Batoche, and in many cases working for the Métis at Batoche, the Lakota Sioux at Moose Jaw supported the Canadian government. Canada had provided them a safe haven from the American army and they didn't want to do anything that would jeopardize their life in Canada.

Superintendent R. Burton Deane (NWMP) reported on his dealing with the Lakota Sioux at Moose Jaw during the Métis Resistance of 1885:

"I now opened negotiations with some Sioux who had been for some time encamped in the neighborhood of Moose Jaw, with a view to engaging them as scouts. I employed, for this purpose, ex-policemen Le Quesne, who is a Sioux interpreter, and had engaged for temporary service as a special constable. These Sioux were adapted for the work, in that they were not in sympathy with the rebels, were very anxious to remain on this side of the line, and were in hopes of inducing the Canadian Government to grant them a reserve. One of the conditions I imposed was that each scout should mount himself, and herein lay the difficulty. It appeared that their ponies had been acquired by the work of the women, whose property they consequently were, and the women objected to the men embarking on any undertaking which might expose them and their families to the vengeance of the other tribes."

"Ultimately, I obtained five Sioux Scouts who kept me informed of what was passing in all the Indian Camps in this district, and I was more than satisfied with the work they did, and with the veracity of their reports, confirmation of some of which I afterwards obtained."

"Runners were constantly on the move between the different camps, inciting their occupants to join the rebels, but it was not possible to arrest them, for want of timely information, the difficulty being greater because I could not run the risk of exposing my scouts to suspicion."

"A half-breed runner tried to persuade the Sioux to rise, with a promise that they should have a share of the country when the Indians should have regained their own, and bribed them to give them information as to police movements, on his return from the south, but he failed to keep his appointment."[50]

Some of the Métis of Wood Mountain and Willow Bunch were also employed by the NWMP. The report of Superintendent Deane continues:

"Mr. Légaré, of Wood Mountain, arrived here (Regina) to represent to the Lieutenant-Governor that a large number of half-breeds at Wood Mountain and Willow Bunch were in starving condition that they wished to remain there, so as not to be implicated in any way with the rebellion, and that they would be glad of any employment. Mr. Légaré, having great influence with these half-breeds, and scouts being urgently required, it was proposed that a given number of them should accept service as scouts under Mr. Légaré's direction ... the selection, of course, was left to him."

VIII. MOOSE JAW REQUESTS A RESERVE FOR THE LAKOTA

ON October 29, 1886, sixty-eight Moose Jaw residents petitioned Edgar Dewdney (Lieutenant-Governor and Indian Commissioner), requesting a reserve for the Lakota Sioux. It stated: "… your petitioners are residents of Moose Jaw and District, … there are in this neighborhood some Indians that belong to the Sioux … that have been resident in the vicinity for the past two or three years and … we have found them to be uniformly industrious, virtuous and law abiding and are a great convenience to the citizens engaging as they do in all work given to them by the people with zest and faithfulness particularly the female members of the tribe who are valuable aids to the women of the district where female servants are difficult to obtain and we would respectfully request that you as Indian Commissioner assign to them a reserve in the vicinity …"[51]

Lieutenant-Governor/Indian Commissioner Dewdney did not have any sympathy for the Lakota Sioux in Canada. He felt that the participation of some Lakota Sioux in the Métis Resistance of 1885 was good reason to deny all Lakota Sioux any consideration. He wanted their guns and horses taken; and he wanted them forced across the American border.[52] Cooler heads prevailed and no action was taken against the Lakota Sioux; but the petition of the sixty-eight Moose Jaw residents was denied.

In January, 1887, the Mayor of Moose Jaw, J. G. Gordon, along with John Taylor, an interpreter from the Department of Indian Affairs, went to the Lakota Sioux camp at Moose Jaw. Taylor reported: "I endeavoured to obtain a list of names of the men and number of their families but this I was unable to do as they regarded me with great suspicion and refused to give me any information. The reason for this as far as I could learn and from what was told me by Black Bull who is apparently one of their headmen is that some of them had taken part in the massacre of General Custer and his men and they were afraid that I was trying to gather information for the United States Government. I am informed that the people of Moose Jaw had represented them to the Indian Dept., as being destitute and requiring assistance. They replied that they did not want anything to be given to them as they earn money for themselves by hunting and working about the town of Moose Jaw."[53] Taylor observed that there were 100 Lakota Sioux in 30 lodges.[54] In February, 1887, a second Indian Affairs interpreter, Le Quesne, was sent to the camp. He did not obtain any additional information.[55]

IX. BLACK BULL

JOHN MACLEAN, the Methodist missionary previously quoted, reported on the death of Black Bull's son: "During the spring of 1888, the son of the Sioux chief of the Band of Moose Jaw died, and the deceased was placed in a coffin covered with red cloth and deposited upon a platform raised about ten feet in the air, on four stout poles. When the body was placed on the platform, a horse belonging to the deceased was tied by the tail to one of the posts, and shot. I saw the bones of the animal under the scaffold, the dogs having eaten the flesh. A large and small coffin, trimmed alike, were lying on the scaffold."[56] The presence of a small coffin indicates that Black Bull lost a grandchild as well as a son, probably from the same illness.

Tucked away in the Moose Jaw Library archives is the family history of the Mack and Sine Families. Henry Mack was a Baptist Minister in Moose Jaw from April 12, 1892, until December 1, 1893. The family history records: "Here was camped a tribe of Indians who had taken part in the Custer Massacre, Black Bull ... was their Chief. He could speak English fluently; he was a frequent visitor at our home and at these visits held Percy and Harry on his knees calling them 'Papoose'..."[57]

The Mack and Sine family history has a photograph claiming to show Black Bull and Mrs. Black Bull. The same photograph is in three books published in the 1890's.[58] The captioning beneath the photograph is incorrect because it labels the Indian sitting furthest from Mrs. Black Bull as her husband. It would be more likely the Indian sitting next to Mrs. Black Bull is her husband. The photograph labels them "Black Bull Bear" and "Mrs. Black Bull Bear", casting doubt on the identification. Further casting doubt, the photograph is in the Denver Public Library, but with captioning that does not include the names "Black Bull Bear" or "Mrs. Black Bull Bear". For more discussion about the Denver Public Library photograph, see Appendix H (Possible Photograph of Black Bull & Wife).

In the winter of 1892-3, there was a dispute among the Lakota Sioux at Moose Jaw. The Lakota Sioux split into two groups that camped separately around Moose Jaw. One camp continued to be led by Black Bull; the other was led by White Rabbit, also known as Big Jim.[59] One of the camps, probably the one led by White Rabbit, went to Willow Bunch in October, 1893, and wintered there.[60] White Rabbit was a veteran of the Little Big Horn who surrendered with Crazy Horse.[61]

In 1894, Thomas Aspdin, who later became the first Indian Agent of the Lakota Sioux at Moose Jaw, reported on Black Bull's feelings about returning to the United States:

"Referring to the matter of the Sioux leaving for their own country ... I have had a long talk with "Black Bull" (who has always been against going back) and after a considerable time, he told me that, if I would go along with them he would go himself and also the rest. I informed him that I could not promise him that, where upon he told me he would not go, unless he was taken by force. "Broken Leg" (this could be Burnt Thigh aka Brave Heart) also told me the same thing. They have been told by the people in town, that they cannot be moved by force."

"I have known most of them for nearly 20 years and as my wife is Sioux, it is possible they may feel confidence in going over with a white man whom they have known so long. They have great fears of being met by the soldiers and maltreated if going alone."[62]

Gontran Laviolette was a Catholic missionary to the Sioux Indians in Canada. He wrote two books about the Sioux in Canada: *The Sioux Indians in Canada* (1944) and *The Dakota Sioux in Canada* (1991, includes information about the Lakota Sioux). According to Father Laviolette, Black Bull organized a Ghost Dance in 1895. Some Lakota Sioux, including Brave Heart, had learned about the new religion on visits to reservations in the United States. The dance took place at a fork of Wood River, six miles northwest of the present town of Gravelbourg.[63]

Black Bull deserves greater recognition. He was seriously wounded at the Little Big Horn. He led his people while they adapted to Canadian life at Moose Jaw; and he was a spiritual leader, sponsoring a Ghost Dance in Canada. Black Bull died in 1897 and was buried near Moose Jaw.[64]

In 1910 the widow of Black Bull (Tasinaskawin) died at Moose Jaw. She was buried in the old Moose Jaw cemetery by Annie (Smith) Wallis. Annie came to Moose Jaw in 1890 as a young woman.[65] She became friends with the Lakota Sioux and compiled a Lakota dictionary that is in the archives of the Moose Jaw Library. The Lakota Sioux gave her many gifts that can now be seen in the Moose Jaw Museum, next to the library.

Mrs. Black Bull rests in the southwest corner of the old Moose Jaw cemetery near the south fence (Appendix I, Grave of Tasinaskawin). Her headstone reads: "Tasinaskawin, BRULÈ, Died Apr. 3, 1910". The words are enclosed by a "sheriff shield" design, similar to the badge appearing in the photograph discussed on page 13 and shown in Appendix H.

X. NWMP REPORTS 1887-1894

MOST of the NWMP annual reports from 1887 to 1894 mention the Lakota Sioux in Canada, especially the "Moose Jaw Sioux". Here are excerpts from the reports:

1887, E.W. Jarvis: "A few Sioux Indians, from the neighborhood of Moose Jaw, camped at Wood Mountain and at Willow Bunch at different times during the summer. They were quiet and gave no trouble whatever."[66]

1888, E.W. Jarvis: "Most of the Sioux Indians from Moose Jaw came south to the Pinto Horse Butte (40 miles west of the Wood Mountain Post) early in the summer on a hunting expedition, and worked their way to Wood Mountain, near which they camped until the end of August, when the majority of them returned to Moose Jaw."

"Indian runners from Standing Rock agency, Montana (sic), U.S., visited the Sioux camp at Wood Mountain and at Moose Jaw. Their object was to induce our Indians to join them in case of the outbreak of hostilities across the line, but as far as I could learn they did not succeed in getting any promises."

"During the time these Indians were in the district they behaved very well, and gave us no trouble whatever."[67]

1888, A.B. Perry: "There are about 170 Sioux Indians (Dakota) living in the vicinity of Prince Albert (35 miles northeast of Batoche), who have no treaty, and obtain a living without the assistance of the Government. They came here from eleven to twelve years ago, and have since earned a precarious living by working about the towns and in the country, and by hunting. They are mostly Minnesota Sioux (Dakota), who came to Canada after the (Minnesota War) … A few are Tetons (Lakota), who came over with Sitting Bull … They now live in a small village (since 1894, Reserve #94A – Wahpeton) on the north side of the Saskatchewan, near the Little Red River. They are hard working and moral. Some have expressed a wish to settle on a reserve, where they could engage in farming. Although so close to the town, they are all heathens and receive no christian teaching whatever. There are about thirty-five children, who should be attending school, but are growing up like their parents."

1888, A.B. Perry (continued): "The hope of improvement in the Indian, lies in the training of the rising generation, and it is hoped that before long the children will be taken in hand."

"This is my third annual report in which I have been able to speak of the very good conduct of the native population. Not a single crime has been committed amongst them. Intending immigrants need entertain no apprehension whatever of them, and may feel confident of the safety of their families, and the security of their property.[68]

1889, E.W. Jarvis: "The Moose-Jaw Sioux paid their annual visit to Wood Mountain, spending most of the summer there."[69]

1891, P.C.H. Primrose: "Most of the Sioux Indians who live at Regina and Moose Jaw during the winter spend the summer in this vicinity (Wood Mountain), in order to hunt and keep their ponies out of the settlers crops. They give no trouble."[70]

1892, A.C. Macdonell: "The Sioux Indians living around the post (Wood Mountain) are American Indians, and efforts were being made last spring to send them across the line. They give us little or no trouble, but as they are living a-hand-to-mouth existence in Moose Jaw in the winter, and at Wood Mountain in the summer, to keep their ponies out of the settlers' crops and to hunt, as the supply of game diminishes, they have yearly greater temptation to kill cattle, etc. As an instance of the amount of game they kill, a party of four men returned from a hunt in August last with seventy-two antelope."[71]

1892, A.B. Perry: "This irregular band of Sioux Indians is still living about Moose Jaw and Wood Mountain. They came into Canada in 1877 and have lived an independent though precarious life since that time. They have obeyed the laws of the country and lived peacefully."

"No attempt has been made to place them under control, or confine them on a reserve, and it is probable that if such an attempt were made they would exhibit considerable impatience, and would be difficult to manage. There are twenty-eight families, nine widows - in all, with children, one hundred and fifteen souls. At least fifty-five of these children have been born since their entry into Canada. They own over one hundred ponies."

1892, A.B. Perry (continued): "The future of these people demand attention. Are they to be allowed to become permanent residents, or are they to be induced or forced to return to the United States? They now maintain themselves by hunting chiefly. They kill a great deal of game. Inspector Macdonell mentions that they brought, at one time, seventy-two antelope into Wood Mountain Post. I know of another instance where one camp killed ninety-nine. Such wholesale slaughter will have its effects."

"A certain number work about Moose Jaw cutting wood and doing odd jobs. If the Government of the United States will receive these Indians back and give them the same treatment as the others, it would be greatly to their advantage to send them. Their children are growing up without education, or any training which might help them earn a living."

"The general impression is that they would not go back to the States willingly. I believe that it is in their own interests and to the advantage of this district that they be returned to their own land."[72]

1893, A.B. Perry: "There was some petty quarrelling amongst the Sioux Indians at Moose Jaw last winter. The majority of the camp moved last October to Willow Bunch, where they will winter. They live in their cotton tents summer and winter, and during the extreme weather of January and February, they must suffer a great deal. No attempt has been made, as yet, to locate them on a reserve, or to return them to their own country. For their own sakes some action should be taken. I dealt more fully with this subject in my last year's report ..."[73]

1894, W.H. Routledge: "A small number of American Sioux Indians, who have lived in Canadian territory for a number of years, camped near the post (Wood Mountain) during the summer. They spend their time between Moose Jaw and Wood Mountain, and are a harmless lot. It is to be regretted that they cannot be persuaded to return to the United States territory, or failing that, settle on a reserve on this side of the line – the latter course mainly in the interest of their families."[74]

1894, A.B. Perry: "47 of the refugee Sioux living about Moose Jaw were induced to return to the U.S. last spring by the Indian Department, who furnished them with rations for the journey. They were well received by the American authorities. However, 2 families returned to Canada this fall. They stated they had been well treated, but preferred to live in Canada."[75]

17

XI. SOME LAKOTA SIOUX RETURN TO THE U.S. (1889-1895)

At the time of Sitting Bull's surrender in 1881, the largest Sioux reservation in the United States, the Great Sioux reservation, occupied almost the entire western half of what is now South Dakota. The Black Hills, and land to the north and south of the Black Hills, had been carved out of the reservation in 1876. Under the Dawes Act of 1887 and the Sioux Act of 1888, each Sioux family head was offered 160 acres and the Sioux Nation would give up the remaining reservation land for $0.50 an acre. The reservation would be reduced by half. For land cessions to take effect, the Fort Laramie Treaty of 1868 required that 75% of the adult males on the reservation give their consent. The Sioux refused to consent.

The American government tried again. The Sioux Act of 1889 offered each Sioux family head 320 acres and the Sioux Nation would give up the remaining reservation land for $1.25 an acre.[76] Knowing that Congress was fully capable of confiscating their land, as it had done with the Black Hills, 75% of the adult Sioux males on the reservation gave their consent. The final signatures needed to implement the Sioux Act of 1889 were obtained at Standing Rock agency on August 3, 1889.[77] Standing Rock was the agency where Sitting Bull had been brought in 1883 and he was opposed to any land cessions. The Sioux at Standing Rock withheld their consent until the government agreed to compensate them for the horses that were taken as a result of the 1876 war; and also agreed to the extension of the school provisions of the 1868 Fort Laramie Treaty.[78]

Under the Sioux Act of 1889, the land remaining to the Great Sioux reservation was divided into six Sioux reservations: Standing Rock, Cheyenne River, Lower Brulé, Crow Creek, Pine Ridge and Rosebud. For any Lakota Sioux in Canada thinking about returning to the United States, the prospect of obtaining 320 acres under the Sioux Act of 1889 was a factor for them to consider; and the Canadian government gave travel assistance to Lakota Sioux who returned to the United States.[79]

A number of Lakota Sioux in Canada went to reservations in the United States and made land claims; some returned to Canada after their land claim was secure or simply because they liked Canada better. The NWMP report for 1892 indicated there were 115 Lakota Sioux in 28 families: 115/28 = 4.1 per family. For the years 1889-1895, I use 4.1 as the average family size to calculate population movements when a source refers to a number of Lakota Sioux "families" or "lodges".

BLACK MOON THE MNICOUJOU CHIEF

I have mentioned Black Moon, the Hunkpapa Chief who returned to the United States prior to the return of Sitting Bull. I have also mentioned a Mnicoujou Chief named Black Moon. Both Chiefs supported Sitting Bull's rise to leadership and both Chiefs were present at the Little Big Horn.[80] In 1875, the Mnicoujou Black Moon was one of eight prominent Mnicoujou leaders. He was a shirt-wearer (head councilor); someone entitled to wear the true scalp shirt.[81] He was also called "Loves War".[82]

Black Moon/Loves War stayed in Canada after Sitting Bull surrendered in July, 1881. His daughter, Mary Black Moon, married Thomas Aspdin (NWMP), sometime after May 1, 1881.[83] His granddaughter, Emma Loves War, married Okute Sica (Hard to Shoot) and they founded the LeCaine family. Another granddaughter, Katrine Loves War, married Big Joe Ferguson (He Killed Two) and they founded the Ferguson family. The marriages of the granddaughters took place in 1889.[84]

During the days prior to April 26, 1889, eleven lodges (44 people) of Lakota Sioux left Moose Jaw for the United States.[85] Thomas Aspdin was instrumental in persuading the Lakota they would be better off among their people in the United States. The most prominent man in the group was Black Moon/Loves War. Also in the group were his relations through marriage, Okute Sica (Hard to Shoot) and Big Joe Ferguson (He Killed Two). The families of Okute Sica (3 people) and Big Joe Ferguson (2 people) returned to Canada in the fall of 1889.[86]

The fact that Okute Sica (LeCaine family) and Big Joe Ferguson chose Canada over the United States is very important to the history of the Lakota in Canada. Of 208 registered band members, as of Feb. 10, 2004, at least fifty were LeCaine's and at least twenty-five were Ferguson's. The fact that Okute Sica and Big Joe Ferguson were married to sisters who were granddaughters of Black Moon/Loves War, a prominent Mnicoujou Chief, enhances the standing of the Lakota Sioux in Canada (Appendix J, Granddaughters of Black Moon, The Mnicoujou Chief).

Because of the importance of Black Moon/Loves War in the history of the Lakota Sioux who remained in Canada, I will give a detailed account of his return to the United States and what happened to his family during the last years of his life. These events are well documented, partly due to written inquiries made to American Indian agents by Thomas Aspdin, the son-in-law of Black Moon.

19

On June 4th, 1889, U.S. army headquarters in Washington D.C. received a telegram from Fort Buford. It reported that on June 2nd, U.S. Cavalry intercepted thirty-one Sioux men, women and children, "Black Moon" the principal man, at the crossing of the Missouri River, near the Berthold agency, Dakota Territory. The telegram advised that what few arms they had were taken and recommended the Indians be allowed to proceed, unescorted, to Standing Rock reservation.[87] The Black Moon group was detained pending instructions from Washington.

On June 18, 1889, Washington ordered Fort Buford to allow Black Moon and his party to proceed to Standing Rock reservation, without guard of military or Indian police.[88] Black Moon arrived at Standing Rock in July, 1889 and enrolled at that agency. Including himself, there were twelve people in his family, four men, four women, two boys and two girls.[89] Black Moon arrived at Standing Rock just as the land cession under the Sioux Act of 1889 was being hotly debated.

While at Standing Rock the Black Moon family lived on the Grand River.[90] Sitting Bull also lived on the Grand River. It is impossible to believe the two chiefs did not meet. Any Lakota returning from Canada and going to Standing Rock, or passing through on their way to one of the Lakota reservations further south, most likely would have met with Sitting Bull and exchanged family news.

On August 13, 1890, three more families (12 people) left Moose Jaw for Standing Rock (Appendix K, Letter of Hayter Reed). Among them was Seechah (The Thigh). Seechah was associated with the Brulé and Oglala branches of the Lakota Sioux.[91] He may have intended to visit Rosebud or Pine Ridge reservations; if so, events stopped him. He saw Sitting Bull and Black Moon at Standing Rock but returned to Canada with his family (four people) in 1891.[92] His return was important to the Lakota remaining in Canada because Seechah, also known as Brave Heart, later became the last "old time" chief of the Lakota at Wood Mountain.

Black Moon decided to leave Standing Rock to live with his people, the Mnicoujou, at Cheyenne River reservation. He received permission from James Mclaughlin, the influential Indian agent at Standing Rock, and arrived at Cheyenne River reservation around November 1, 1890.[93] According to his son, Paul High Back, they went to live among Big Foot's people.[94] Unfortunately, Black Moon was arriving at Cheyenne River reservation and Brave Heart was at Standing Rock, near Sitting Bull, just as the tragic events of the Ghost Dance religion were about to take place.

20

THE GHOST DANCE RELIGION

No one can understand the conversion of many Lakota to the Ghost Dance religion unless they understand the varying degrees of despair that existed among the Lakota Sioux in the United States. Vastly outnumbered, 20,000 Lakota; men, women and children; had to come to terms with the new realities of reservation life. Armed opposition to the white advance had failed, as indeed it was doomed to fail. No hunting and gathering people can defeat an industrial society in armed conflict.

What were the new realities of reservation life? Each reservation had an Indian agent who controlled the distribution of food and other favors. The Indian agents, implementing government policy, wanted the Lakota to live as white farmers. They wanted them to tend to their own individual acreages and raise farm animals. They wanted them to live in houses. They wanted them to send their children to school. At school they wanted the children to speak English and not Lakota. They wanted the Lakota to accept Christianity. They wanted the men to stop having more than one wife. They wanted each Lakota to stay on their particular reservation and not leave unless given permission. They wanted them to submit to record keeping; such as an annual census and a record of goods received by each head of household. Worse of all, they wanted the Lakota men to stop practicing the old ways of distinguishing themselves: warfare, horse raiding, hunting and spiritual quests. Each Indian agency had a fort nearby; there remained the ultimate threat of the American army.

To accomplish their goals the Indian agents needed to diminish the authority of traditional chiefs, traditional spiritual men and traditional tribal elders; and needed to prop up Indian leaders who seemed to be supportive of the agent. Indian agents were politically appointed. Each reservation was a Byzantine world of white politics, tribal politics, traditionalists, modernists and opportunists; each in all shades and all degrees. It was hard for Lakota to decide what road was best.

Sad accommodations were made. Some Lakota were allowed to "hunt" the cattle for their beef allotment.[95] Some Lakota lived far enough from their allotment station so that they were constantly on the move, going to the station or away from it.[96] A Lakota man could earn some warrior honors by joining the Indian reservation police. There were significant differences between the reservations. The main variable was the strength of the traditional tribal leaders versus the strength of the Indian agent.

At Standing Rock reservation, where many Hunkpapas lived, Sitting Bull was the leader of the traditionalist Indians; but his opponent was one of the strongest and most intelligent of the Indian agents – James McLaughlin. McLaughlin's wife was one quarter Dakota Sioux. He took a paternalistic attitude towards Indians, but sincerely believed their best interests were served by governmental policy. A plus for McLaughin was that he had a streak of fairness in him; as when he advocated that the Lakota be compensated for horses taken in the Sioux War of 1876.[97] His sense of fairness, however, did not extend to Sitting Bull.

At Cheyenne River reservation, adjoining Standing Rock and to the south; the Mnicoujou Chiefs, Big Foot and Hump, were the leaders of the traditionalists. They mainly achieved their purpose by living as far away from the Indian Agent as they could. But Hump had served as a scout for the army and had developed a close relationship with some officers; this won him an appointment to chief of Indian police at Cheyenne River.[98]

At Pine Ridge reservation, southwest of Cheyenne River reservation, many Oglalas lived. At Pine Ridge, Red Cloud found ways to offer passive resistance to the Indian Agent. Red Cloud had the prestige of being the only Indian chief to win a war against the whites; the 1866-68 War along the Bozeman Trail, referred to as Red Cloud's War. But Red Cloud came to recognize the futility of war against the Americans. Even so, he was a thorn in the side of his Indian agent.[99]

At Rosebud reservation, adjoining Pine Ridge and to the east, Spotted Tail was chief of the Brulé Lakota. He did not fight in Red Cloud's war or the 1876 War, but he habitually outmaneuvered his Indian agent; as when he was allowed to appoint Rosebud reservation police. However, Spotted Tail was assassinated by a Brulé Lakota in 1881; and no Brulé with the talent of Spotted Tail was able to rise to leadership.[100]

During 1889 and 1890, the Lakota Sioux at Pine Ridge, Rosebud and Cheyenne River faced additional hardships of hunger, sickness and death; especially the death of many children. Drought affected the region and the crops failed.[101] White settlers were free to move to better land. The Lakota had to stay where they were. To make matters worse, within weeks of the approval of land cessions, the government substantially cut the beef ration.[102] Together with prior cuts, some Lakota were only receiving one half to two thirds of the food they were due under the treaties.[103] Weakened by hunger, the children were more vulnerable to disease and death.[104] It is likely many elders also died.

The land surrender under the Sioux Act of 1889, the new realities of reservation life and the cutting of tribal food rations, all combined to set the stage for the arrival of a new Indian religious movement: the Ghost Dance. In 1889 rumors from the west reached the Lakota about a new messiah who had come to save Indians from their misery.[105] Lakota at Pine Ridge and Rosebud held councils to discuss this matter.[106] The Lakota, and other tribes, sent delegates to learn the truth of the rumors; and to find the messiah, if possible.[107] One of these delegates was Kicking Bear, a headman of the Mnicoujou at Cheyenne River reservation. He was married to a niece of Big Foot.[108] Among the Lakota, Kicking Bear would become one of the most important leaders of the Ghost Dance.

The new messiah was a Paiute Indian named Wovoka, also known as Jack Wilson. Wovoka lived near Yerington, Nevada, and the Walker River Paiute reservation; about ninety miles southeast of Reno. Wovoka gained a reputation as someone who could perform miracles and control the weather. He was also subject to falling into trances and visiting the spirit world; from which he brought back messages from God.[109] He said the messiah, as Christ, had been to earth before, but had been rejected and killed. This time the messiah had come to Indians.[110]

A Northern Cheyenne named Porcupine is the source of the earliest comprehensive statement of Wovoka's teachings; dated June 15, 1890. According to Porcupine, Wovoka said: "My father told me the earth was getting old and worn out, and the people getting bad, and that I was to renew everything as it used to be, and make it better." Porcupine continued: "He told us also that all our dead were to be resurrected; that they were all to come back to earth, and that as the earth was too small for them and us, he would do away with heaven, and make the earth itself large enough to contain us all; that we must tell all the people we meet about these things. He spoke to us about fighting, and said that was bad, and we must keep from it; that the earth was to be all good hereafter, and we must all be friends with one another. He said that in the fall of the year the youth of all the good people would be renewed, so that nobody would be more than 40 years old, and that if they behaved themselves well after this the youth of everyone would be renewed in the spring. He said if we were all good he would send people among us who could heal all our wounds and sickness by mere touch, and that we would live forever. He told us not to quarrel or fight, nor strike each other, nor shoot one another; that the whites and Indians were to be all one people."[111]

Wovoka warned "if any man disobeyed what he ordered, his tribe would be wiped from the face of the earth; that we must believe everything he said, and that we must not doubt him, or say he lied; that if we did, he would know it; that he would know our thoughts and actions, in no matter what part of the world we might be."[112] Some have argued the Lakota changed Wovoka's message to make it specifically hostile to whites, but this view is based on the statements of Indian police who were opposed to the dance. It appears Wovoka, and his Lakota disciples, reserved their punishments for non-believers; a religious doctrine not unique to the Ghost Dance. Of course, when the United States government took harsher and harsher measures to suppress the religion, the level of Indian resentment escalated.[113]

Lakota converts to Wovoka, as well as other plains Indians, believed the renewal of the earth promised by Wovoka meant the return of the buffalo and the rich life provided by good hunting. However, it was not going to be an easy matter for the new world to arrive. Wovoka told his followers they must dance a special dance - the Ghost Dance. They must periodically perform the dance; four consecutive days until midnight and then until sunrise of the fifth day.[114] When a sufficient number of followers were doing the dance, the spirit world would come to earth.

During 1889 and 1890 the Ghost Dance spread rapidly from tribe to tribe across the plains. Its growth was aided by the railroad and the U.S. postal service. Railroad men made little effort to stop Indians from riding the cars. Mail sacks carried letters from believers who proclaimed the good news of the messiah. Educated Indian youth were among those who transcribed and translated the letters for their elders.[115]

Early in 1890 Lakota delegates found the messiah. They came home and preached his religion. Kicking Bear was a key figure in the movement. In Wyoming he had witnessed Arapaho ghost dancing. He had seen dancers fall into a faint whereby they could see and talk with their dead relations.[116] After Kicking Bear reported to the Lakota the excitement could not be contained. At Pine Ridge the dancing began in August, 1890. In September it spread to Rosebud and Cheyenne River reservations.[117] At Cheyenne River, Big Foot and Hump supported the Ghost Dance. Big Foot joined Hump's camp at the mouth of Cherry Creek, north of the Cheyenne River; and they danced together.[118] On October 9th, 1890, at Standing Rock, Kicking Bear arrived at Sitting Bull's camp on the Grand River. He had been invited by Sitting Bull and the dancing soon began.[119]

Explaining the new religion, Red Cloud said: "We felt that we were mocked in our misery. We had no newspapers and no one to speak for us. We had no redress. Our rations were again reduced. You who eat three times each day, and see your children well and happy around you, can't understand what starving Indians feel. We were faint with hunger and maddened by despair. We held our dying children, and felt their little bodies tremble as their souls went out and left only a dead weight in our hands. They were not very heavy, but we ourselves were very faint, and the dead weighed us down. There was no hope on earth, and God seemed to have forgotten us. Some one had again been talking of the son of God, and said he had come. The people did not know; they did not care. They snatched at the hope. They screamed like crazy men to Him for mercy. They caught at the promises they heard he had made."[120]

At Pine Ridge forty percent of the Indians were dancing; at Rosebud, thirty percent; at Cheyenne River, fifteen percent; at Standing Rock, ten percent.[121] Settlers feared the dancing was a prelude to an armed Lakota uprising. Sensational, and false, newspaper stories made matters worse. The agent at Pine Ridge, Daniel Royer, began to beg for military intervention.[122] On November 20, 1890 the army occupied Pine Ridge and Rosebud. Lakota from both reservations fled to the "Stronghold" in the badlands of Pine Ridge; The Stronghold had steep cliffs, two springs for water, grass for forage and a narrow approach; all ideal for defense.[123]

On December 12, 1890 Colonel Drum, the military commander at Fort Yates, received orders from General Miles to arrest Sitting Bull.[124] Soon after, agent McLaughlin received a poorly translated message from Sitting Bull stating that he wanted to go to Pine Ridge.[125] The government feared Sitting Bull would rally more Lakota to the Stronghold. On December 15, 1890, McLaughlin and Drum sent Indian police, backed by U.S. Cavalry, to arrest Sitting Bull. A gunfight broke out with Sitting Bull's followers and Sitting Bull was killed.[126] His age was no more than fifty-nine.[127]

After Sitting Bull was killed hundreds of his people, angry and fearful, fled south to the Cheyenne River. Among them was The Thigh (Brave Heart). They found Hump and Big Foot near the mouth of Cherry Creek. By this time Hump had turned against the Ghost Dance and he urged everyone to surrender at Fort Bennett.[128] Hump's advice was followed by almost all of his people; most of the Sitting Bull refugees, including The Thigh[129]; and some of Big Foot's people, including Black Moon. Tragically, some of Black Moon's family stayed with Big Foot.[130]

On December 22, 1890, Big Foot was at his settlement south of the Cheyenne River at the mouth of Deep Creek. His band numbered at least 333 people, including 38 from Sitting Bull and 30 from Hump.[131] The most die-hard traditionalists and Ghost Dancers from Sitting Bull, Hump and Big Foot were concentrated in this camp. Army units were nearby to the west and east. Under pressure from his headmen, Big Foot agreed to seek the protection of Red Cloud at Pine Ridge; 150 miles to the south.[132]

On December 28, 1890, Big Foot was intercepted by the army and both sides camped. The number in Big Foot's band had increased to 370.[133] The next day, while the band was being searched for weapons, a shot rang out and the Wounded Knee Massacre began; 200-300 Indians were killed; men, women and children.[134] Black Moon lost a wife, a son and a daughter. His son, Paul High Back, was wounded (Appendix L, Letter From Cheyenne River Agent to Aspdin). Another son, Philip Black Moon, was present but escaped injury.[135] Wounded Knee inflamed the situation at the Pine Ridge reservation; but on January 15, 1891, Kicking Bear surrendered and the Sioux "Outbreak" was over.[136]

In the annual Cheyenne River census each family was given a number it retained the next year. New arrivals were put at the end of the list. In the 1891 census, the newly arrived Black Moon was given the census number of Chief Big Foot, killed at Wounded Knee. This indicates the importance of Black Moon during the last years of his life. Agency records indicate Black Moon died March 1, 1893.[137] From census records his age was 72.

In May, 1894, forty-seven Lakota Sioux left for the United States; but two families (8 people) returned to Canada in the fall.[138] Of the remaining 39; seventeen were Hunkpapa and ended up at Standing Rock, twenty-two were Mnicoujou and ended up at Cheyenne River.[139] Included among the Mniconjou were Mary Black Moon, her three daughters, her mother, her sister and a grandson of Black Moon.[140] Mary, her daughters and mother returned to Canada in August, 1895 (5 people returning to Canada).[141]

In early December, 1895, three families, including 11 people, left for the United States; but one of these families (4 people) returned to Canada.[142] The net loss to Canada, due to all the reported trips to the United States, was 88 Lakota. Where did all these Lakota Sioux come from? At various times there were Lakota populations reported at Wood Mountain, Willow Bunch, Fort Qu'Appelle, Moose Jaw, Regina, Moose Woods, Batoche and Prince Albert. The Lakota Sioux who returned to the United States could have come from any, or all, of these locations.

XII. INDIAN AGENT REPORTS 1900-1910

IN 1900, Thomas W. Aspdin, formerly of the NWMP, was assigned the task of supervising the "Moose Jaw Sioux". As previously mentioned, his wife was Mary Black Moon, the daughter of the Mnicoujou Chief. In 1894, Mary was in the group that went to the United States, but she returned to Canada in 1895. Thomas Aspdin died on February 9, 1906. In 1913, Mary permanently relocated to Cheyenne River reservation.[143]

Aspdin joined the NWMP at its inception in 1873. He was promoted to Corporal in July, 1878. In August, 1878, he was assigned the task of surveying the Lakota Sioux at Wood Mountain. On May 1, 1881, Aspdin was promoted to staff sergeant and posted at Wood Mountain as acting quartermaster. During this period Tom and Mary were wed, following Indian custom. Aspdin visited Moose Jaw in 1883 and 1884; he moved to Moose Jaw in 1888.[144] Aspdin and his wife were very familiar with the Lakota Sioux who lived between Moose Jaw and the American border.

The winter of 1895-96, Aspdin allowed the Lakota Sioux to camp on his property, just south of Moose Jaw. On April 28, 1896, he wrote to the Department of Indian affairs requesting payment for the use of his land.[145] He was in serious financial difficulty at this time. His land yielded poor crops and cattle prices were low. The interest rate on his mortgage was 18%. Aspdin could not make the payments and the bank foreclosed.[146]

In 1897, Aspdin was appointed "Farmer in Charge" of the Assiniboine reserve located 100 miles east of Moose Jaw (Reserve #76 – Carry-the-kettle).[147] In 1901, Aspdin was made the Indian Agent at Carry-the Kettle; in 1906, W. S. Grant was appointed Indian Agent; in 1912, Thomas E. Donnelly was appointed Indian Agent. Here are their reports from 1900-1910 regarding the Moose Jaw Sioux:

INDIAN AGENT ASPDIN

September 6, 1900; Sioux:

"In April I received word from the Indian Commissioner that the camp of refugees at Moosejaw had been attached to this agency for supervision, with instructions to visit them periodically."

"This camp is made up of broken remnants of the Sioux who came over to Canada in the years 1876 and 1877. They have been around Moosejaw since 1883."

"They number about 125 souls. Both men and women work around Moosejaw and for the settlers in harvest time, and make a good living, but in their present condition are not likely to make homes for themselves. Whilst fairly well behaved, the life around town is beginning to show, and some of them have cultivated a taste for liquor. I had one man convicted and fined for supplying liquor, and have taken steps to check it as much as possible."

Some of the Indians have put their children to school, and it is to be hoped others will follow. Others of the Indians in the camp, I regret to say, are very abusive to those who have sent their children to school, and subject them to a kind of persecution in the camp. It is a question whether it might not be expedient to use drastic measures a little to stop this."[148]

August 2, 1901; Sioux Band, Moosejaw:

"These Indians came over from the United States at the time of the hostilities with the American government."

"In the year 1876 they were attacked by General Custer ...

"Many of the Sioux (numbering at one time about six thousand Indians) came to this side (Canada), and made their hunting-grounds around Wood Mountain and Cypress Hills (140 miles west of Wood Mountain) for some years, where they were effectually controlled by a handful of the Northwest Mounted Police."

"Many returned in time to their agencies in the States, and the remainder, about the time of the disappearance of the buffalo, and contemporaneously with the building of the Canadian Pacific Railway, moved to the town of Moosejaw, and have made a living ever since working for settlers, selling bead-work, etc."

"They number about 125 and their life around the town tends a good deal to lead them to bad habits."

"Temperance. – They get liquor without much trouble, and although a white man and an Indian were convicted lately for supplying it, which will tend to check it, I fear from their close proximity to town that they will still get some."

"Health. - At one time they were very healthy, but of late years tuberculosis in one form or another has become very prevalent."

"Characteristics and Progress. – While some of these Indians earn considerable money by working around, they are making no permanent progress, and live in tents both winter and summer."[149]

August 4, 1902; Sioux Band, Moosejaw:

"These Indian came over from the United States in 1876-77 with Sitting Bull."

"They number about 120, and make a living around Moosejaw, Wood Mountain and Willow Bunch. It would be better for them if they were settled on some reserve. Living as they do, at large, their habits have not improved, and around Moosejaw they got in to the way of getting a good deal of liquor. Since taking them under supervision, I have had several convictions against persons supplying them, which has had a good effect in checking it. These Indians, although making a living, are not improving and the prospects are not bright for them in this respect unless they become settled on some place of their own."[150]

August 15, 1903; Sioux (Moosejaw):

"These Indians still continue to make a living around Moosejaw and vicinity. They do not, however, get anything ahead and are not making any improvement. They would do better if they could be persuaded to go to some place where they could make permanent improvements."[151]

August 15, 1904; Moosejaw Sioux:

"These Indians, commonly called the Moosejaw Sioux, are a remnant of Sitting Bull's band who came from the United States during the hostilities in 1876-7. For some years they hunted about Wood Mountain and with the disappearance of the buffalo, came to Moosejaw, making a living by doing work around town, selling beadwork, etc. Whilst they do not receive much from the government, they are non-progressive, living in tents the year round. Some of them are fond of liquor and notwithstanding that several persons have been fined for supplying liquor to them, they no doubt still get it frequently. They would be better settled on a reserve away from the town."

"The population of the Sioux at Moosejaw and vicinity is 112."[152]

June 30, 1905; Moose jaw Sioux:

"These are a remnant of the camps of Sioux who came to Canada in 1877 in consequence of the hostilities between them and the American government. At first they hunted in the vicinity of Wood Mountain. Afterwards on the disappearance of the game to subsist on, they came to Moose Jaw and earned a living working for the white people."

"Whilst their behavior on the whole has been good, they make no improvements and live in tents the year round."

"After a careful census, their numbers are as follows: 37 men, 34 women, 22 boys and 26 girls, or 119 in all."[153]

INDIAN AGENT GRANT (1)

June 30, 1906: The new Indian agent, W. S. Grant, does not mention the Moose Jaw Sioux in his first report.[154]

March 31, 1907; Moosejaw Sioux:

"Position. - "The Moosejaw Sioux are non-treaty Indians having no reserve, inhabiting the country from Moosejaw to the boundry (U.S)."

"Population. – There are approximately 112 people in this band."

"Occupations. – These Sioux labor for the settlers and for the people of Moosejaw. Some of them are good butchers and others tanners. Many of them still gain a livelihood by hunting."

"Abode. – These Indians have no permanent houses, but live in tents at all seasons of the year."

"Stock. – Many of these Sioux have numerous ponies for sale and their own use."

"Education. – A number of these Indians speak English quite well. None of their children are attending any of the industrial schools."

"Characteristics and Progress. – These Sioux are hard workers and independent, having learned to shift for themselves. They apparently earn a good living. Their mode of dress is much like that of white men."

"Temperance and Morality. – Though in proximity of town, these Indians get very little liquor, due to the vigilance of the Royal Northwest Mounted Police. I have heard no complaint against their morality."

"Health. - The health of these Sioux is robust, there having been but one death amongst them during the year. Drs. Turnbull and McCullagh are in medical attendance on these Indians."[155]

March 31, 1908; Moosejaw Sioux:

"Position. - The Moosejaw Sioux are non-treaty Indians without a reserve, inhabiting the country from Moosejaw to the boundry (U.S.)."

"Population. – The population of this band is estimated to be 115 persons."

"Occupations. – These Sioux work as farm-laborers for the settlers in the neighborhood of Moosejaw. Some of these Indians work for the townspeople of Moosejaw. Their wives do tanning, along with odd jobs about the town. Others almost wholly depend upon hunting for a living."

"Abode. – They live in tents throughout the year and pitch camp wherever night overtakes them."

"Stock. - The Sioux were unable to realize much money on the sale of their ponies during the year."

"Education. – From their peculiar position, the Sioux have acquired enough English to make themselves understood. They seem to be prejudiced against sending their children to school."

"Progress. – The Sioux of necessity have learned to shift for themselves. A few of the old people had to be helped with rations during the early part of this winter."

"Health. – There have been several cases of small pox amongst these Indians during the summer."

"Drs. Turnbull and McCullagh are in medical attendance on these Indians."[156]

March 31, 1909; Moosejaw Sioux:

"Position. - The Moosejaw Sioux are non-treaty Indians without a reserve, inhabiting the country from Moosejaw to the boundry (U.S. border)."

"Population. - The population of this band is estimated to be 117 persons."

"Abode. – They have not any permanent houses, but live in tents throughout the year."

"Occupations. – Some of the Sioux Indians make a living by working for the settlers in the neighborhood of Moosejaw, and also the people of the town. Their wives do tanning, scrubbing, washing, along with other odd jobs about the town. Others depend almost entirely upon hunting for a livelihood."

"Stock. – The Sioux have numerous ponies for sale and for their own use. During the past year they were able to realize a little more money on the sale of their ponies than the year before."

"Education. - A number of the Sioux can speak fairly good English. This is due to their peculiar position. They do not seem to be inclined to send their children to school."

"Progress. – These Sioux are good workers and independent, having learned to shift for themselves. A few of the old people had to be helped with rations during the month of March."

"Health. - The health of these Indians has been very good. Only one death occurred amongst them during the year. Drs. Turnbull and McCullagh are in medical attendance on these Indians."[157]

March 31, 1910; Moosejaw Sioux:

"Position. – The Moosejaw Sioux are non-treaty Indians without a reserve, inhabiting the country between Moosejaw to the boundry (U.S.)."

"Population. – The population of this band is estimated to be 121 persons."

"Buildings. – They have no permanent houses, but live in tents throughout the year."

"Occupations. – The Sioux Indian are good workers and independent, having learned to shift for themselves. Some of them make a living by working in the town of Moosejaw; others work for settlers in the neighborhood of the above mentioned town. Others again depend altogether upon hunting for a livelihood. There are a few old people that have to be assisted."

"IIealth. - The health of these Indians has been good."[158]

NOTE: The Indian Agent Reports of the Department of Indian Affairs are in the Sessional Papers of Canada, as are the reports of the North-West Mounted Police. Every large Canadian library has the Sessional Papers.

XVIII. MORE REQUESTS FOR A CANDIAN RESERVE

ON April 27, 1893, *The Regina Leader* reported: "The Sioux Indians south of town (Moose Jaw) have petitioned the Government for a reserve. They have quite a number of horses and with proper management might be made self sustaining." This petition resulted because of a conflict with the farmers around Moose Jaw, caused by Lakota Sioux horses getting into the farmers' crops. The petition was denied, but the Canadian government offered the Lakota Sioux rations if they would remove their horses to Wood Mountain during harvesting. The Lakota Sioux agreed, but declined the offer of rations, not wanting to be dependent on the government, and thus coming under its control.[159]

As the land around Moose Jaw become populated the Lakota Sioux found it more difficult to find places to camp and to keep their horses. On November 20, 1903, Moose Jaw was incorporated as a city, having a population of around 3,200 people.[160] The 1906 census gave Moose Jaw a population of 6,249.[161] In 1907, the Percy Cassidy Company, the owners of the land on which the Lakota Sioux were camping, asked the Department of Indian Affairs to purchase the land for the Lakota Sioux. The company had wanted to sell the land, but the Lakota Sioux were quarantined there because of several cases of small pox during the summer. The Department of Indian affairs did not act on the request, but pressure was building to remove the Lakota Sioux from Moose Jaw.[162]

A. D. Pringle was a Presbyterian student missionary who homesteaded east of Limerick from 1908 until 1912.[163] In June, 1909, he suggested to the Department of Indian Affairs that the Lakota Sioux be given a reserve in Wood Mountain, about 25 miles southwest of Limerick, near the site of the old NWMP post. This was where the Lakota Sioux went in 1876 and where some Moose Jaw Sioux visited during summers. Due to frontier marriages, it was an area the Lakota Sioux never completely left. Land to the west of the Wood Mountain Post had not yet been surveyed and opened to homesteading. Reverend Pringle wanted something done for the Lakota Sioux before the land was taken.[164] He also said the Lakota Sioux should be given the right to homestead. In 1907, John LeCaine, a Lakota Sioux, moved west of the old NWMP post. He homesteaded there in 1910, but used the name of his mother's first husband, a white man.[165]

XIV. SITTING BULL'S PEOPLE GET A RESERVE IN CANADA

ON October 29, 1910, the Canadian government set aside an area essentially three miles by six miles (18 sq. miles/11,520 acres) west of the Wood Mountain mounted police post, as a temporary reserve for the Lakota Sioux. In 1919 the western half of the reserve was taken away from the Lakota Sioux and opened to settlement for veterans of World War I.[166] On August 5, 1930, the reserve was made permanent at a size of 8.25 sq. miles/5,280 acres (Appendix M, Order in Council No. 1775). The Hudson's Bay Company (HBC) owned three quarter-sections (0.75 sq. miles/480 acres) in the center of the reserve. On October 7, 1930, the Hudson's Bay Company surrendered this land to the reserve, increasing its size to 9.0 sq. miles/5,760 acres.[167]

In February, 1954, John Okute LeCaine made his homestead (0.25 sq. miles/160 acres) part of the reserve, increasing it to 9.25 sq. miles/5,920 acres; he then legally became a member of the Wood Mountain Band.[168] Access to the reserve is a gravel road 1.2 miles south of the Village of Wood Mountain, running west from Highway 18. From the highway, it is one mile to the reserve boundary and 3.5 miles to the tribal office. (Appendix N, Map of Wood Mountain Indian Reserve No. 160).

The Indian Agent Reports of 1911-1916, and the population statistics I have compiled in Appendix O, indicate the majority of the Lakota Sioux never lived year round on the reserve. In the Indian Agent reports the Lakota Sioux are still referred to as the "Moose Jaw Sioux", even when most no longer wintered at Moose Jaw. In the history of the reserve, the largest gathering of Lakota Sioux took place during the summer of 1912; the Royal North-West Mounted Police (RNWMP) reported 130 Lakota Sioux at Wood Mountain "On temporary reserve; not self-supporting"[169] (Appendix O, Lakota Sioux at Moose Jaw and Wood Mountain).

XV. INDIAN AGENT REPORTS 1911-1916

THE Indian Agent reports of 1911 and 1915 incorrectly state that the Lakota Sioux did not have a reserve. This may be because their reserve had "temporary" status. Another explanation is that many of the Lakota Sioux continued to roam and gave no indication they would settle full-time on the reserve. Ultimately, the Canadian government based the permanent size of the reserve on the number of Lakota Sioux who settled there year round and its notion of how much land each Indian family should have. Here are the Indian Agent Reports from 1911-1916:

INDIAN AGENT GRANT (2)

April 17, 1911; Moosejaw Sioux:

"Position. – The Moosejaw Sioux are non-treaty Indians without a reserve inhabiting the country from Moosejaw to the boundary (U.S.)."

"Population. – The population of this band is estimated to be 124."

"Health and Sanitation. – The health of these Indians has been good. Their wandering habits secure for them the benefit of the natural sanitation and prevent the accumulation of refuse. Dr. Turnbull and McCullagh are the medical attendants for them."

"Abode. – They live in tents throughout the year, as they have no permanent houses."

"Occupations. – These Indians work for the people of Moosejaw and for the settlers. Many of them gain a livelihood by hunting."

"Stock. – They have a large number of ponies for their own use and for sale."

"Characteristics and Progress. – These Sioux are good workers and independent, having learned to shift for themselves. Their mode of dress is like that of white people."

"Temperance and Morality. – Though these people live near the town, they get very little liquor, due to the vigilance of the town constable. I have heard no complaints against their morality."[170]

INDIAN AGENT DONNELLY

April 23, 1912; Moosejaw Sioux:

"Position. – The Moosejaw Sioux are non-treaty Indians, inhabiting the country from Moosejaw to the boundary (U.S.)."

"Population. – The population of this band is estimated to be 124."

"Health and Sanitation. – These Indians continue the old custom of living under canvas, as they are frequently changing their localities, it secures for them the benefit of the natural sanitation and prevents the accumulation of refuse."

"Occupations. – These Indians work for the people of Moosejaw, and for the settlers. A number of them depend on hunting and trapping for a livelihood."

"Stock. – The Sioux have numerous ponies for sale and for their own use."

"Characteristics and Progress. – These people are good workers and independent, having learned to shift for themselves. Their mode of dress is like that of the white people."

"Temperance and Morality. – These people get very little liquor, though they live near the town, due to the vigilance of the town constable."[171]

April 30, 1913; Moosejaw Sioux:

"Position. – The Moosejaw Sioux are non-treaty Indians, inhabiting the country from Moosejaw to the boundary (U.S.)."

"Population. – The population of this band is estimated to be 124."

"Health and Sanitation. – These Indians continue their old customs of living in tents, as they are roaming from one place to another nearly all the time. During the year not many families remained in the vicinity of Moosejaw. They were mostly scattered. Being a nomadic people they secure for themselves the benefit of natural sanitation, thus preventing the accumulation of refuse."

"Occupations. – These Indians work for the farmers and ranchers at Wood Mountain. Some of them work for the citizens of Moosejaw. A number of them depend on hunting and trapping for a livelihood."

"Stock. – The Sioux have a large number of ponies for sale over and above what they need for their own use."

"Characteristics and Progress. – These people are good workers considering the roaming condition they are in. They are independent, having learned to shift for themselves. Their mode of dress is much like that of the white people."

"Temperance and Morality. – These people indulge very little in liquor. This I believe is due mostly to the great efforts put forth by the Royal Northwest Mounted Police stationed at Wood Mountain and Moosejaw, also by the city police at Moosejaw. Only one case was tried for drinking liquor. Their moral habits are considered good."[172]

1914 (no precise date); Moosejaw Sioux:

"Health and Sanitation. – These Indians live in tents throughout the year. Being a nomadic people, they escape the accumulation of refuse."

"Occupations. – Some get employment in towns at different occupations. Others work for farmers and ranchers. Some depend on trapping and hunting for a livelihood."

"Stock. – They have a good stock of ponies, and usually sell what they do not use. From these sales they realize fair sums of money."

"Temperance and Morality. These Indians are quite temperate. Their morals are considered good."

"Characteristics and Progress. – Owing to their roaming nature, these Indians are not making progress that other bands are."

"Many of the young men are good workers, having learned to rely on their own resources from the time they were old enough to do so. The mode of the men is similar to that of white men, but the women continue to wear the blanket."[173]

1915 (no precise date); Moosejaw Sioux Band:

"The people of this band are non-treaty Indians inhabiting the country between Wood Mountain and Moosejaw, the majority living at Wood Mountain."

"Health and Sanitation. – They live in tents throughout the year. Being nomads, they are enabled to remove from unsanitary surroundings."

"Occupations. – Many of them get employment in towns at different occupations; others depend on trapping and hunting for a livelihood; some work for farmers and ranchers. Some of the women make moccasins and other Indian wares."

"Stock. – They have a good stock of horses, and take fairly good care of them."

"Temperance and Morality. – These Indians may be considered temperate in their habits. Their morals are good."

"Characteristics and Progress. – These people are not making the progress that they should. Matters might be different if they were settled on a reserve of their own. (NOTE: These statements, and Appendix O, indicate a majority of the Lakota Sioux didn't live full-time on the reserve. Some probably maintained a free roaming lifestyle even into the 1920's.) These Indians are good workers and industrious. The mode of dress of the men is similar to that of the white men; but the women still cling to the blanket. Some of them can speak English, but only a few are educated."[174]

1916 (no precise date); Moosejaw Sioux:

"These people are non-treaty Indians. Some live at Wood Mountain, others in the city of Moosejaw, while others live in the various small towns between these two places."

"Occupations. – Many of these people work for farmers and ranchers. Others have settled on a small reserve at Wood Mountain and are raising horses. A few spend a portion of their time hunting."

"Buildings. – They do not possess many buildings, but live mostly in tents."

"Health and Sanitation. – They appear to be healthy, and do not require very much medical attention."

"Temperance and Morality. – These people are temperate in their habits. The R.N.W.M. Police stationed at Moosejaw and Wood Mountain keep a close watch over them. They inform me from time to time that they have no trouble with them. Their morals are good."[175]

XVI. BRAVE HEART

B RAVE HEART, a veteran of the Battle of the Little Big Horn, was Chief when the Wood Mountain reserve was created. He was born around 1857 and died in 1934.[176] John Okute LeCaine and Pete Lethbridge then acted as spokesmen.[177] In 1968, William Goodtrack was elected Chief.[178] In 2005, Ellen LeCaine was elected Chief. In 2009, David Ogle was elected Chief. In 2012, Travis Ogle was elected Chief. Biographies of about 50 Wood Mountain Lakota are posted on the internet.[179]

Most of what we know about Brave Heart is from the writings of John Okute LeCaine.[180] Brave Heart, also known as Thigh, was a Brule (Burnt Thigh) of the "Red Cloud Oglala", This means he could have been a Wazhaza (sub-group of Oglala who were of Brule origin). Brave Heart lost both parents at an early age. As an adult he took the name of his father. There was a lower Brule named Brave Heart who signed the Fort Laramie Treaties of 1866 and 1868[181]; and then disappears from history. Perhaps the two Brave Hearts are father and son. Brave Heart was visiting the United States, living near Sitting Bull, during the time of the Ghost Dance and the killing of Sitting Bull. His observations of the Ghost Dance had to be the basis for Black Bull's Ghost Dance in Canada in 1895.

In 1910, among the Lakota Sioux, there were 4 Roman Catholics, 6 Presbyterians and 111 "Pagans".[182] In 1945, a small Roman Catholic Chapel was dedicated on the Wood Mountain Reserve.[183] The Lakota Sioux practiced a mixed religion of Roman Catholic and Traditional Religion. (Appendix P, Canadian Dept. of Indian Affairs – Statistics).

XVII. FORT PECK RESERVATION, MONTANA

A FTER the Lakota Sioux came to Canada they kept contact with the Indians living near Fort Peck agency at Poplar Creek, Montana Territory; sixty miles south of the U.S. border. By doing this they were sometimes able to obtain food and supplies. In his surrender speech, Sitting Bull said: "I have many people among the Yanktonais at Popular Creek … I do not wish to leave here (Fort Buford) until I get all the people I left behind (in Canada) and the Hunkpapas now at Poplar Creek."[184] In 1888, Fort Peck agency became Fort Peck reservation. The Wood Mountain Lakota Sioux still have friends and relations at Fort Peck reservation in Montana (Appendix Q, Some Populations on the Northern Plains).

XVIII. THE WOOD MOUNTAIN STAMPEDE

DURING the weekend of the second Sunday in July, the oldest rodeo in Canada takes place: The Wood Mountain Stampede.[185] Many people who have moved away from Wood Mountain return for the rodeo, and for the party that takes place each night. The rodeo grounds are 3.5 miles south of the Village of Wood Mountain and west of the main road, Highway 18. Behind the rodeo grounds there is a regional park for campers and a swimming pool. Food is served at the rodeo and also at the regional park.

THE RODEO-RANCH MUSEUM

THE entrance to the rodeo grounds is also the entrance to the Rodeo-Ranch Museum. It's run by the Wood Mountain Historical Society, which sponsors special events during rodeo weekend. The museum is the single best source of information on the Wood Mountain Lakota Sioux, including their participation in the rodeo. The museum sells its own unique publications about Wood Mountain and the Lakota Sioux in Canada.

THE OLD POST (1874-1918) MUSEUM

A half mile south of the rodeo grounds, the Saskatchewan park service has rebuilt two buildings on the site of the old mounted police post. Photographs of Wood Mountain Lakota Sioux are on display. The site of the original North West Mounted Police post at Wood Mountain is nearby.

XIX. MEMORIAL AND SIOUX UNITY RIDES

IN the winter cold of 1986, 19 Lakota rode horses 150 miles from the Cheyenne River to Wounded Knee, "Big Foot's Trail". Each winter more riders came. The ride increased to 250 miles, starting at the site of Sitting Bull's killing on the Grand River. The ride has become an annual event.[186]

In 1993, a Sioux unity ride went from the Standing Rock reservation to the Birdtail Dakota reserve in Manitoba. Lakota, Nakota and Dakota rode united for the first time since Sitting Bull. In 1996, a Sioux unity ride started at the Wahpeton Dakota reserve near Prince Albert and passed through the Wood Mountain Lakota reserve. It continued to the Big Horn Medicine Wheel and Bears Tipi (Devils Tower) in Wyoming.

XX. THE WOOD MOUNTAIN MEMORIAL TO SITTING BULL

IF you climb the small hill behind the Rodeo-Ranch Museum, you will find a memorial to Sitting Bull and his people in Canada. Wash-té.

XXI. THE WOOD MOUNTAIN LAKOTA TODAY

THE number of people living on the reserve has settled at about a dozen; but registered band membership has been growing and at the end of 2012 totaled 270[187]. The Lakota Sioux in Canada remain a cohesive group who have been through many tough times together. In recent years the Lakota Sioux have strived to preserve their traditional Lakota culture. They have built a band office and a community center. They have re-established contact with their numerous relatives at the Cheyenne River Lakota Nation in South Dakota. They have also begun a powwow, held each summer.

Wood Mountain Lakota families take a keen interest in the history and welfare of their people: Ferguson, Goodtrack, Lecaine, Lethbridge, Ogle, Sherwin, Thomson, Anderson, Brown, and others. Because of these families, there will be more to be written about the Lakota in Canada.

XXII. PEPPERMINT'S HILL

IN the Rodeo-Ranch Museum you can find a dusty binder entitled "Scrapbook" that contains some of the writings of John Okute LeCaine, Wood Mountain Lakota Sioux leader and historian for his people. He concludes, as I shall conclude, with these words:

"Look to the hills, southeast of the Town of Wood Mountain and your eyes cannot evade one particular hill … white pioneers have named this hill "The Three Mile Butte" but to Sitting Bull and his followers, who made Wood Mountain their refuge, it was known by the name of "Peppermint's Hill". Many years ago upon this hill a warrior stood. His name was Peppermint … in a loud voice he was pleading and praying for peace for his war weary people. Three days and nights without food or water, he stands exposed to all the elements, pleading for a moments revelation. Peppermint has vanished … only remnants - ghosts of his kind you have seen … Peppermint's Hill alone stands today bearing these secrets … and there it will stand - mystifying those who will follow us."[188]

ENDNOTES

1. Paul L. Hedren, <u>Sitting Bull's Surrender at Fort Buford: An Episode in American History</u>, 1997 (Fort Union Association, RR 3 Box 71, Williston, ND 58801), page 30.
2. Ibid., page 29.
3. <u>Opening Up The West, 1874-1881, The Official Reports of the North-West Mounted Police</u>, Facsimile Edition, 1973 (Coles Publishing Company), Appendix E for 1877, page 28. F.C. Wade, <u>The Surrender of Sitting Bull</u>, The Canadian Magazine, Vol. XXIV, No. 4, (February, 1905), page 336 & note on page 344. Bonnie Day & Thelma Poirier, <u>Wood Mountain Lakota</u>, 1997 (Saskatchewan Heritage Foundation, 1919 Saskatchewan Dr., 9th Floor, Regina, SK S4P 4H2, Canada, phone: (306)787-4188), page 20. The Saskatchewan Heritage Foundation will photocopy this manuscript.
4. See 3, above, <u>Opening Up The West, 1974-1881</u>, Appendix E for 1877, page 31.
5. See 3, above, <u>Opening Up The West, 1974-1881</u>, Appendix E for 1877, page 32.
6. Robert M. Utley, <u>The Lance and the Shield: The Life and Times of Sitting Bull</u>, 1993 (Henry Holt and Company, Inc.), page 179.
7. See 3, above, <u>Opening Up The West</u>, Appendix D for 1877, page 20; Appendix E for 1877, page 33. Joseph Manzione, <u>I Am Looking to the North for My Life</u>, 1994 (University of Utah Press), page 36. See 6, above, pages 182-183.
8. See 6, above, page 200, referring to the <u>Bismarck Tribune</u>, December 20, 1877.
9. E.A. Brininstool, <u>Chief Crazy Horse, His Career And Death</u>, Nebraska History Magazine, Vol. XII, No. 1, January-March, 1929, page 56, quoting Indian Agent James Irwin, <u>Commissioner of Indian Affairs, Annual Report, 1878</u>, pages 36-37. Kingsley M. Bray, <u>We Belong to the North</u>, Montana, The Magazine of Western History, Vol. 55, No. 2, Summer, 2005, pages 41-45; and <u>Crazy Horse, A Lakota Life</u>, 2006 (University of Oklahoma Press), Chapter 30, Owning a Ghost, pages 395-397.
10. See 6, above, page 200.
11. See 6, above, pages 218-220.
12. E.H. Allison, <u>Surrender of Sitting Bull</u>, 1892, reprinted in South Dakota Historical Collections, Vol. VI, 1912, page 265, part of footnote 15, Report of Major Ilges.
13. See 6, above, page 220.
14. See 6, above, page 222.
15. See 1, above, page 17.
16. See 3, above, <u>The Surrender of Sitting Bull</u>, page 340 and note on page 344.
17. <u>Poplar Poles and Wagon Trails</u>, 1998 (Willow Bunch Historical Society, Box 1995, Willow Bunch, Saskatchewan S0H 4K0, Canada), Vol. 2, pages 789-790.
18. <u>Jean Louis Légaré v U.S.</u>, RG 123, U.S. Court of Claims, Gen. Jurisdiction Case file #15,713, Box 811, 16E3/3/30/2, U.S National Archives, Washington, D.C. The "485" figure is in a handwritten itemized bill found in the court file. This bill is in the published court opinion, but the "485" figure is missing.
19. See 3, above, <u>Wood Mountain Lakota</u>, page 35. <u>They Came To Wood Mountain</u>, 4th Edition, 1995, page 22 by William Lethbridge; Thelma Poirier, Ed., <u>Wood Mountain Uplands from the Big Muddy to the Frenchman River</u>, 2000, Chapter Five, The Lakota, by Elizabeth Thomson and Rory Thomson, page 72; both books are published by the Wood Mountain Historical Society, Box 53, Wood Mountain, SK S0H 4L0, Canada. Gontran Laviolette, <u>The Dakota Sioux in Canada</u>, 1991 (DLM Publications), photograph of Teal Duck and caption, supplied by William Lethbridge.
20. <u>Jean Louis Légaré v U.S.</u>, 24 U.S. Court of Claims Reports 513, 515-516 (1889).

21 Ibid.

22 See 1, above, page 11. See 6, above, page 226.

23 See 20, above, page 516.

24 See 1, above, pages 17, 33. See 20, above, Ibid.

25 E.R. Phaneuf, Hoof-Beats On The Frontier, The Leader-Post, Regina, Saskatchewan, November 27, 1937, reprinted in Big Muddy Badlands Just North of the 49th, 1994, ("Big Muddy Nature Centre & Museum" Committee, Big Beaver, Saskatchewan S0H 0G0, Canada), pages 12-13. The book is sold at the General Store in Big Beaver. For the exact number of Métis scouts (the number became inflated with the passage of time), see 18, above, Deposition of Jean Louis Légaré.

26 See 17, above, Vol. 1, pages 414, 595; Conversation with Randy Gaudry, a great grandson of André Gaudry, at Willow Bunch, Saskatchewan, in 2001.

27 This is my conclusion. For Hunkpapa, Oglala, Brulé and Mnicoujou, see 3, above, Wood Mountain Lakota, page 27 and 19 above, Wood Mountain Uplands, page 72.

28 See 18, above, Deposition of Légaré.

29 See 17, above, pages 737-739.

30 No Neck surrendered with someone identified as Black Horn, but later identified as Black Moon. It seems this Black Moon returned to Canada because he disappears from the ration issue rolls after July 29, 1884. Ration Issue Rolls, Standing Rock agency, May 20, 1884 through July 29, 1884. No Neck is also mentioned in 12, above, Surrender of Sitting Bull, page 250 and in 18, above, Deposition of Légaré. No Neck's wife is listed as a widow in the 1885 census for Standing Rock.

31 Bruce Fairman, Moose Jaw - The Early Years, 2nd Edition, 2001 (HomeTown Press, Moose Jaw, Saskatchewan), pages 1-3, 39, 65.

32 Ibid., page 115. Brian A. Brown, Opening Tomorrow's Doors, 1984 (One hundredth Anniversary Committee of Moose Jaw School District Number One), pages 9-32. North-West Territories Gazette, Vol. 1, No. 2, January 19, 1884.

33 Sessional Papers of Canada, 1901, Report of the Department of Indian Affairs, 1900, Indian Agent Reports, Thomas W. Aspdin, page 128. Leith Knight, all the moose …all the jaw, 1982 (Moose Jaw 100), pg. 11, quoting a letter from Private O'Donnell.

34 John Peter Turner, The North-West Mounted Police 1873-1893, 1950 (Ottawa), Volume 1, page 413. Légaré also says that No Neck and Black Bull were chiefs at Willow Bunch at the time Sitting Bull returned to the United States. See 18, above, Deposition of Légaré.

35 See 12, above, pages 232, 251, 270. The Sioux of Early Moose Jaw Days, Interview With Annie Wallis on May 4, 1956, Moose Jaw Public Library archives, pages 3-4. She says Black Bull was a nephew of Sitting Bull but this is denied by Ernie LaPointe, the great grandson of Sitting Bull and author of Sitting Bull, His Life and Legacy.

36 John Maclean, Canadian Savage Folk, The Native Tribes of Canada, Facsimile Edition, 1971 (Coles Publishing Company), pages 108-109.

37 See 3, above, Wood Mountain Lakota, page 35. See 19, above, Wood Mountain Uplands, page 72, and The Dakota Sioux in Canada, photograph of Teal Duck.

38 Gabriel Dumont, translated by G.F.G. Stanley, Dumont's Account of the North-West Rebellion, Canadian Historical Review, XXX, September 3, 1949, page 259.

39 Walter Hildebrandt, The Battle of Batoche, Revised Edition, 1989 (Canadian Parks Service), pages 17, 20, 23, 31-32, 66 and endnotes. I have added ten Indians to the total to account for Lakota Sioux and Saulteaux participation.

[40] See 19, above, <u>The Dakota Sioux in Canada</u>, photograph of Teal Duck and caption. For Red Bear and Poor Crow (Lean Crow), see 19, above, <u>Wood Mountain Uplands</u>, page 84. The ages of Poor Crow and Red Bear at the Little Big Horn can be determined from 3, above, <u>Wood Mountain Lakota</u>, pages 139, 141. Also for Poor Crow, see 19, above, <u>They Came To Wood Mountain</u>, page 22, by W. Lethbridge

[41] For Black Bull, see 35, above, <u>The Sioux of Early Moose Jaw Days</u>, Ibid. For He Killed Two, see John Okute-Sica, <u>Last of the Old Sioux Dies at Wood Mountain</u>, The Leader-Post, May 8, 1953, Regina, Moose Jaw Public Library archives. If Black Bull was not with the Métis, I doubt if young He Killed Two (17 years old) was with them.

[42] Robert A. Sherlock, <u>1885 Experiences of the Halifax Battalion in the North-West</u>, Reprinted by Museum Restoration Service, 1985 (Jas. W. Doley), pages 13 and 21.

[43] See 33, above, all the moose … all the jaw, page 11, letter from Private Tupper.

[44] See 3, above, <u>Wood Mountain Lakota</u>, page 37. See 19, above, <u>Wood Mountain Uplands</u>, pages 72-73. Conversation with Leonard Lethbridge, a great grandson of Red Bear, in 2005. Leonard lives at the Wood Mountain reserve.

[45] Bob Beal & Rod Macleod, <u>Prairie Fire, The 1885 North-West Rebellion</u>, 1994 (McClelland & Stewart Inc.), pages 306-309. <u>Loyal Till Death, Indians and the North-West Rebellion</u>, 1997 (Fifth House LTD), pages 224-225, 261-263.

[46] <u>Sessional Papers of Canada, 1886</u>, No. 52, QUEEN VS. "WHITE CAP", testimony of Gerald Willoughby, pages 45-51.

[47] See 19, above, <u>The Dakota Sioux in Canada</u>, page 255. Peter Douglas Elias, <u>The Dakota of the Canadian Northwest</u>, 2002 (Canadian Plains Research Center, University of Regina), page 173.

[48] See 47, above, <u>The Dakota of the Canadian Northwest</u>, page 180.

[49] See 3, above, <u>Wood Mountain Lakota</u>, page 37. See 19, above, <u>Wood Mountain Uplands</u>, page 73.

[50] <u>Settlers and Rebels, 1882-1885, The Official Reports of the North-West Mounted Police</u>, Facsimile Edition, 1973 (Coles Publishing Co.), Appendix D for 1885, pg. 63.

[51] Kirk Goodtrack, <u>Wood Mountain Lakota Sioux Legal Submission, Claims to Compensation for Lands 1870 Imperial Order in Council</u>, June 14, 2004, submitted to the Department of Indian Affairs, page 221, citing petition dated October 29, 1886, PAC RG 10, Vol. 3599 File 1564 Pt. A. and PAC RG 10 Vol. 3652 File 8589 Pt. 1.

[52] See 3, above, <u>Wood Mountain Lakota</u>, pages 40-41. See 19, above, <u>Wood Mountain Uplands</u>, page 74.

[53] See 51, above, page 172, referring to John Taylor, <u>Report to the Indian Commissioner</u>, January 18, 1887. RG-10, Vol. 3652, File 8589, pt. 2.

[54] See 3, above, <u>Wood Mountain Lakota</u>, page 41, referring to John Taylor, <u>Report to the Indian Commissioner</u>, January 18, 1887. RG-10, Vol. 3652, File 8589, pt. 2.

[55] See 3, above, <u>Wood Mountain Lakota</u>, page 41, referring to LeQuesne, <u>Report to the Assistant Indian Commissioner</u>, February 4, 1887. RG-10, Vol. 3652, File 8589, pt. 2.

[56] See 36, above, page 116.

[57] <u>The Mack and Sine Families</u>, Family Histories, Moose Jaw Library Archives, pg. 15.

[58] Ibid., page 71. W. Fletcher Johnson, <u>Life of Sitting Bull and History of the Indian War of 1890-91</u>, 1891 (Edgewood Publishing Company), page 73. James P. Boyd, <u>Recent Indian Wars, Under the Lead of Sitting Bull and Other Chiefs</u>, 1891 (Publishers Union), page 142; reprinted 2000 (Digital Scanning, Inc.). James P. Boyd, <u>Red Men on the War Path</u>, 1895 (J. H. Moore Company), page 92.

[59] See 3, above, <u>Wood Mountain Lakota</u>, page 39, referring to Inspector Constantine, To Commanding Officer, July 23, 1892, RG-10, Vol. 3652, File 8589, pt. 2.
See 19, above, <u>Wood Mountain Uplands</u>, pages 73-74.

[60] <u>Sessional Papers of Canada, 1894</u>, Report of the North-West Mounted Police 1893, Appendix C, page 42; quoted on page 17 of this book.

[61] See 19, above, <u>They Came To Wood Mountain</u>, page 22, by William Lethbridge. <u>The Crazy Horse Surrender Ledger</u>, 1994 (Nebraska State Historical Society), page 157.

[62] See 51, above, page 172, referring to Thomas Aspdin, <u>Letter to the Indian Commissioner</u>, April 3, 1894, RG-10, Vol. 3652, File 8589, pt. 2.

[63] Gontran Laviolette, <u>The Sioux Indians in Canada</u>, 1944 (Marian Press), pgs. 119-120. For Brave Heart's knowledge of the Ghost Dance see 92, below, Ibid.

[64] See 35, above, <u>The Sioux of Early Moose Jaw Days</u>, Ibid.

[65] Ibid.

[66] <u>Law and Order, 1886-1887, The Official Reports of the North-West Mounted Police</u>, Facsimile Edition, 1973 (Coles Publishing Company), 1887, Appendix J, page 88.

[67] <u>The New West, The Official Reports of the North-West Mounted Police</u>, Facsimile Edition, 1973 (Coles Publishing Company), 1888, Appendix J, pages 111-112.

[68] Ibid., 1888, Appendix H, page 95.

[69] Ibid., 1889, Appendix J, page 98.

[70] <u>Sessional Papers of Canada, 1892</u>, Report of the North-West Mounted Police, 1891, Appendix E, page 54.

[71] <u>Sessional Papers of Canada, 1893</u>, Report of the North-West Mounted Police, 1892, Appendix D, page 80.

[72] Ibid., Appendix D, page 50.

[73] See 60, above, Ibid. Quoted on page 17 of this book.

[74] <u>Sessional Papers of Canada, 1895</u>, Report of the North-West Mounted Police, 1894, Appendix C, page 87.

[75] <u>Sessional Papers of Canada, 1895</u>, Report of the North-West Mounted Police, 1894, Appendix C, page 52.

[76] Louis L. Pfaller, O.S.B., <u>James McLaughlin, The Man With an Indian Heart</u>, 1992 (Assumption Abbey Press), pages 116, 120.

[77] See 6, above, page 278.

[78] See 76, above, page 120.

[79] See 3, above, <u>Wood Mountain Lakota</u>, page 42.

[80] Stanley Vestal, <u>Sitting Bull, Champion of the Sioux</u>, 1957 (University of Oklahoma Press), pages 92, 143.

[81] Joseph White Bull, <u>Lakota Warrior</u>, 1996 (University of Nebraska Press), pgs. 31-32.

[82] My thanks to Gus LeCaine for John LeCaine's note about Black Moon/Loves War.

[83] Maggie Siggins, <u>Revenge of the Land</u>, 1991 (McClelland & Stewart. Inc.), pages 77-110. Siggins confuses the two Black Moons. <u>Aspdin to Commissioner of Indian Affairs</u>, June 5, 1890 (Document 21681, Letters Received, Office of Indian Affairs, RG-75, National Archives), McLaughlin Papers, microfilm roll 34, State Historical Society of N.D., Bismarck, ND. Aspdin said he lived with his wife, her sister and her mother. He described Black Moon as a Mnicoujou, very tall and 60-70 years old.

[84] <u>Indians of Moose Jaw, Emma</u>, by George LeCaine, son of Emma, January 17th, 1969 and <u>Indians of Moose Jaw, Big Joe</u>, by George LeCaine, nephew of Big Joe, January 17th, 1969; Moose Jaw Public Library archives, Sioux Indians.

[85] Thomas Aspdin, Letter to Hayter Reed, Moose Jaw, April 26, 1889, RG-10, Vol. 3599, File 1564, pt. A.

[86] See 19, above, They Came To Wood Mountain, page 22. See 83, above, both sources.

[87] Assistant Adjutant Gen., Division of Missouri, to Adjutant Gen., U.S. Army, June 4, 1889, McLaughlin Papers, microfilm roll 33. State Historical Society of N.D., Bismarck, ND. Ephriam D. Dickson III, Black Moon: The Minnecoujou Leader, Little Big Horn Associates Newsletter,Volume 40, No. 10, December, 2006, pgs. 4-5. The detained group had 49 horses. I think some of the Moose Jaw group evaded the army.

[88] Adj. Gen., U.S. Army, to Commanding General, Division of Missouri, June 18, 1889, McLaughlin Papers, microfilm roll 33. State Historical Society of N.D., Bismarck, ND

[89] James McLaughlin, Indian Agent, Standing Rock to Indian Agent, Cheyenne River, October 14, 1890, McLaughlin Papers, microfilm roll 21, frame 358. State Historical Society of N.D., Bismarck, ND. The 1890 Standing Rock census lists the Black Moon family but with errors. Comparing this census with the 1891 Cheyenne River census and the letter in 92, below, I have made a better family list. The four men were: Black Moon, age 69; Two Spears (Two Lance), son, age 25; White Dog, son, age 20; High Back (Paul), son, age 19. The four women were: Red Lodge, wife, age 46; Rattling Wind, wife, age 76; Yellow Ear (Brown Ear), daughter, age 25; Jumps (Skip, Jumper), daughter, age 25. The two boys were: Touches Killed (Henry), son, age 14; Many Arrows (Wounded Often, Philip), son, age 11. The two girls were: Taken From Her, daughter, age 15; Spotted Wing (Spotted Horse), granddaughter, age 4.

[90] Ibid.

[91] See 19, above, They Came To Wood Mountain, page 19. John Okute LeCaine, The Stone War Club, Moose Jaw Public Library archives, Sioux Indians.

[92] Eva Wojcik, Trust and Survival: AWOL Hunkpapa Indian Family Prisoners of War at Fort Sully, 1890-1891, The American Indian Quarterly, Volume 32, Number 3, Summer, 2008, pages 275-296, page 287. Major General Miles to Commanding Officer Fort Sully, letters dated May 2, 1891, May 4, 1891 & May 12, 1891. James Mclaughlin Papers, microfilm roll 35. State Historical Society of N.D., Bismarck, ND

[93] Perain P. Palmer, Indian Agent, Letter to Thomas W. Aspdin, August 5, 1891 (Doc. 30470, Letters Received, Office of Indian Affairs, RG-75, National Archives), McLaughlin Papers, microfilm roll 34, State Historical Society of N.D., Bismarck, ND

[94] Paul High Back's Version of the Disaster of Dec. 29, 1890, at Wounded Knee, The Wi-Iyohi, South Dakota Historical Society, Vol. 10, No. 3, June, 1956.

[95] Robert M. Utley, The Last Days of the Sioux Nation, 1963 (Yale University), page 22.

[96] James McLaughlin, My Friend the Indian, 1970 (Superior Publishing Company), The Missing Three Chapters, Chapter 14, How Hawkman Rode to His Death.

[97] Ibid., page 75.

[98] See 95, above, pages 81-82.

[99] George E. Hyde, Red Cloud's Folk, A History of the Oglala Sioux Indians, 1957 (University of Oklahoma Press).

[100] George E. Hyde, Spotted Tail's Folk, A History of the Brulé Sioux, 1974 (University of Oklahoma Press).

[101] George E. Hyde, A Sioux Chronicle, 1956 (University of Oklahoma Press), pgs. 232-233. James Mooney, The Ghost-Dance Religion and the Sioux Outbreak of 1890, reprint of 1896 edition, 1991 (University of Nebraska Press), pages 831-842.

[102] See 95, above, page 55.

[103] See 101, above, <u>A Sioux Chronicle</u>, page 230; and <u>The Ghost-Dance Religion and the Sioux Outbreak of 1890</u>, pages 837, 840-841.

[104] See 101, above, <u>A Sioux Chronicle</u>, page 238. "Captain Sword of the Pine Ridge police told the Reverend Cleveland of Rosebud that in the winter of 1889-90 the Pine Ridge death rate was 25 to 45 a month in a population of some 5,500, most of the victims being small children."

[105] See 95, above, page 60-61. On July 23, 1889, Elaine Goodale, a teacher at Pine Ridge, recorded in her diary: "Chasing Crane, on his way home from Rosebud, is welcomed with supper and a smoke. God, he says, has appeared to the Crows! In the midst of a council he came from nowhere and announced himself as the Savior who came upon earth once and was killed by the white men. He had been grieved by the crying of parents for their dead children, and would let the sky down upon the earth and destroy the disobedient. He was beautiful to look upon, and bore paint as a sign of power. Men and women listen to this curious tale with apparent credence."

[106] See 101, above, <u>The Ghost-Dance Religion and the Sioux Outbreak of 1890</u>, Statements of George Sword and William Selwyn, pages 819-820. Sam Maddra, <u>Hostiles? The Lakota Ghost Dance and Buffalo Bill's Wild West</u>, 2006 (University of Oklahoma Press), Statements of Short Bull, pages 192-193, 210.

[107] See 101, above, <u>The Ghost-Dance Religion and the Sioux Outbreak of 1890</u>, pages 816-820; and 105, above, <u>Hostiles? The Lakota Ghost Dance and Buffalo Bill's Wild West</u>, Ibid.

[108] See 95, above, page 62. David Humphreys Miller, <u>Ghost Dance</u>, 1959 (University of Nebraska Press), page 11.

[109] Edward C. Johnson, <u>Walker River Paiutes, A Tribal History</u>, 1975 (Walker River Paiute Tribe), Chapter IV, The Ghost Dance Prophets (1860-1895), pages 41-57.

[110] See 101, above, <u>The Ghost-Dance Religion and the Sioux Outbreak of 1890</u>, pg. 796.

[111] Ibid.

[112] Ibid.

[113] See 106, above, <u>Hostiles? The Lakota Ghost Dance and Buffalo Bill's Wild West</u>, pages 29-41. Michael Hittman, <u>Wovoka and the Ghost-Dance</u>, 1990 (University of Nebraska Press), page 235, The Chapman Interview. Dated December 6, 1890, this is the earliest white account of Wovoka's teachings. Arthur Chapman was sent by General John Gibbon, Commander of the Pacific Division, to find and interview the "Indian who impersonated Christ".

[114] See 101, above, <u>The Ghost-Dance Religion and the Sioux Outbreak of 1890</u>, pages 780-781.

[115] See 95, above, page 67.

[116] See 101, above, <u>The Ghost-Dance Religion and the Sioux Outbreak of 1890</u>, pages 798, 820. See 93, above, page 84.

[117] See 95, above, page 84.

[118] See 95, above, pages 131.

[119] See 6, above, page 283.

[120] James P. Boyd, <u>Recent Indian Wars Under the Lead of Sitting Bull, and Other Chiefs</u>, 1891 (Publishers Union), pages 180-181; reprinted 2000 (Digital Scanning, Inc.), but with a typographic error ("they did not care" becomes "they did not dare").

[121] See 95, above, page 112.

[122] See 95, above, pages 109-111.

[123] See 95, above, page 122.

[124] See 6, above, page 295.

[125] See 6, above, page 296. See 94, above, page 152.

[126] See 6, above, pages 295-301; and 94, above, pages 152-160.

[127] See 6, above, page 3.

[128] See 95, above, pages 131-132. Hump surrendered to General Miles in 1877 and became a scout for the army. For seven years he served under Captain Ezra P. Ewers. On November 28, 1890, General Miles ordered Captain Ewers transferred from Texas to Dakota Territory, to see Hump. Captain Ewers asked Hump to stop dancing and to bring his people to Ft. Bennett. Hump agreed and on December 9, 1890, he arrived at Fort Bennett with the vast majority of his people. Some remained behind at Cherry Creek. Big Foot returned to his settlement at Deep Creek.

[129] See 92, above. Around 250 Sitting Bull refugees surrendering at Fort Bennett were taken across the Missouri River to Fort Sully on Dec. 30, 1890 and sent back to Standing Rock, May 16, 1891 (in custody for 4 ½ months). The Thigh (Brave Heart) was allowed to return to Canada. His detainment was never written about in Canada.

[130] See 93, above and Richard E. Jensen, Big Foot's Followers at Wounded Knee, Neb. History, Vol. 71, No. 4 (Winter, 1990), page 204, names listed under High Back.

[131] See 95, above, page 179. See 101, above, A Sioux Chronicle, page 296; and The Ghost-Dance Religion and the Sioux Outbreak of 1890, page 865. Eli S. Ricker, The Indian Interviews of Eli S. Ricker, 1903-1919, 2005 (University of Nebraska Press), pages 194-195.

[132] See 95, above, pages 184-185. See 101, above, A Sioux Chronicle, page 297; and The Ghost-Dance Religion and the Sioux Outbreak of 1890, pages 865-866. See 130, above, The Indian Interviews of Eli S. Ricker, 1903-1919, pages 194-195. Big Foot had promised to meet with the army to discuss bringing his people to Fort Bennett. There are a number of explanations as to why he headed for Pine Ridge. One explanation is that John Dunn, a local rancher, sent by the army to persuade Big Foot to go to Fort Bennett, panicked the Indians by telling them the army would attack if they did not go to Fort Bennett.

[133] See 101, above, A Sioux Chronicle, page 299. See 130, above, Big Foot's Followers at Wounded Knee, page 195.

[134] See 130, above, Big Foot's Followers at Wounded Knee, page 198.

[135] Ibid., pages 201-212. This is a list of Indians said to be at Wounded Knee, compiled from all known sources. Some Black Moon family members are listed under the name of his son, High Back, but the information is not totally accurate. More accurate information is found in the letter referenced in 93, above (Appendix L of this book). Black Moon said that Philip Black Moon, age 12, was sent to the "boys boarding school" (quotation marks used by the Indian agent). However, Black Moon arrived at Cheyenne River around November 1, 1890, while the Ghost Dance was at its peak. The schools were closed due to poor attendance and the general turmoil. At least one witness places Philip at Wounded Knee. See James H. McGregor, The Wounded Knee Massacre From the Viewpoint of the Sioux, 1940 (James H. McGregor), statement of Alice Dog Arm, page 114; and Philip Black Moon told McLaughlin he was at Wounded Knee. See McLaughlin Papers, microfilm roll 17, Notebook 40, page 10, State Historical Society of North Dakota, Bismarck, ND.

[136] See 95, above, page 261.

[137] The Black Moon family kindly shared this information with me and I thank them. In July, 2005, four great grandchildren of Black Moon, Norma, Gabe, David and Norvan, traveled with me to Wood Mountain, Saskatchewan, where they met their Canadian relatives for the first time. The Black Moon name is still used in Canada.

[138] See 75, above, Ibid. Quoted on page 17 of this book.

[139] Peter Couchman, Indian Agent, Cheyenne River to James McLaughlin, Indian Agent, Standing Rock, dated July 12, 1894, General Correspondence, Box 23, Kansas City Regional Branch, National Archives. My thanks to Kingsley Bray for this letter.

[140] South Dakota's Ziebach County, History of the Prairie, 1982 (Ziebach County Historical Society, Dupree, SD), Cris and Kate Aspdin Williams, pages 635-636. Included is a letter to the Indian agent at Fort Peck reservation, Montana:

Regina, May 7th, 1894

Sir:

The bearers of the present communication are some of the United States Indian Sioux refugees who have lived in the neighborhood of the town of Moose Jaw in the North West Territories of Canada since the year 1877 and who are now returning to their country.

From correspondence with the Indian Commissioner at Washington, it is assumed that you will have been notified to be on the look out for them, and have instructions to direct them to their respective reservations, where they will receive the rations and clothing to which they are entitled along with the other members of their respective bands.

On the authority of your Government they have been assured that they would be welcomed back and kindly treated by its officials.

Assistant Commissioner of Indian Affairs

[141] See 83, above, Revenge of the Land, page 100. For the year of return (1895), see Report of Aspdin to the Indian Commissioner, Moose Jaw, September 26, 1895, RG-10, Vol. 3599, File 1564, pt. B.

[142] See 3, above, Wood Mountain Lakota, page 42, referring to Aspdin to Indian Commissioner, Moose Jaw, December 5, 1895, RG-10, Vol. 3599, File 1564, pt. B.

[143] See 83, above, Revenge of the Land, pages 109-110.

[144] See 83, above, Revenge of the Land, pages 63-94.

[145] Aspdin to Indian Commissioner, Moose Jaw, April 28, 1896, RG-10, Vol. 3599, File 1564, pt. B.

[146] See 83, above, Revenge of the Land, pages 96-103.

[147] See 83, above, Revenge of the Land., page 104.

[148] Sessional Papers of Canada, 1901, Report of the Department of Indian Affairs, 1900, Reports of Superintendents and Agents, page 128.

[149] Sessional Papers of Canada, 1902, Report of the Department of Indian Affairs, 1901, Reports of Superintendents and Agents, pages 117-118.

[150] Sessional Papers of Canada, 1903, Report of the Department of Indian Affairs, 1902, Reports of Superintendents and Agents, page 114.

[151] Sessional Papers of Canada, 1904, Report of the Department of Indian Affairs, 1903, Reports of Superintendents and Agents, page 135.

[152] <u>Sessional Papers of Canada, 1905</u>, Report of the Department of Indian Affairs, 1904, Reports of Superintendents and Agents, page 127.

[153] <u>Sessional Papers of Canada, 1906</u>, Report of the Department of Indian Affairs, 1905, Reports of Superintendents and Agents, page 102.

[154] <u>Sessional Papers of Canada, 1906-7</u>, Report of the Dept. of Indian Affairs, 1906, Reports of Superintendents and Agents, pages 113-114.

[155] <u>Sessional Papers of Canada, 1907-8</u>, Report of the Dept. of Indian Affairs, 1907, Reports of Superintendents and Agents, page 109.

[156] <u>Sessional Papers of Canada, 1909</u>, Report of the Department of Indian Affairs, 1908, Reports of Superintendents and Agents, pages 117-118.

[157] <u>Sessional Papers of Canada, 1910</u>, Report of the Department of Indian Affairs, 1909, Reports of Indian Agents, page 124.

[158] <u>Sessional Papers of Canada, 1911</u>, Report of the Department of Indian Affairs, 1910, Reports of Indian Agents, page 114.

[159] See 3, above, <u>Wood Mountain Lakota</u>, page 42, referring to RG-18, Vol. 84F, File 465-1893.

[160] <u>Moose Jaw Times-Herald</u>, June 25, 1953, Jubilee Supplement, page 30.

[161] <u>1906 Census of the Northwest Provinces</u>. Section for Saskatchewan.

[162] See 3, above, <u>Wood Mountain Lakota</u>, page 59, referring to RG-10, Vol. 7779, File 27137-1.

[163] Gontran Laviolette ,<u>The Sioux Indians in Canada</u>, 1944 (Marian Press), page 123, note 15. <u>Prairie Trails and Pioneer Tales</u>, 1982, (Limerick Historical Society), pages 541-542.

[164] See 3, above, <u>Wood Mountain Lakota</u>, page 59.

[165] See 19, above, <u>Wood Mountain Uplands</u>, page 78. See 3, above, <u>Wood Mountain Lakota</u>, pages 60, 91. The 1910 date: email from the <u>Saskatchewan Archives Board</u>.

[166] See 19, above, <u>Wood Mountain Uplands</u>, pages 76-78. See 3, above, <u>Wood Mountain Lakota</u>, pages 60-62.

[167] Email from the <u>Saskatchewan Archives Board</u> (referring to Ottawa file 27137-1). The Saskatchewan Archives Board has the land ownership history for each quarter-section in Saskatchewan.

[168] Letter from John Okute LeCaine to Ray Glasrud dated May 3, 1961. Ray Glasrud, Shaunavon, Saskatchewan

[169] <u>Sessional Papers of Canada, 1913</u>, Report of the North-West Mounted Police, 1912, page 165.

[170] <u>Sessional Papers of Canada, 1912</u>, Report of the Department of Indian Affairs, 1911, Reports of Indian Agents, page 122.

[171] <u>Sessional Papers of Canada, 1913</u>, Report of the Department of Indian Affairs, 1912, Reports of Indian Agents, pages 131-132.

[172] <u>Sessional Papers of Canada, 1914</u>, Report of the Department of Indian Affairs, 1913, Reports of Indian Agents, page 128.

[173] <u>Sessional Papers of Canada, 1915</u>, Report of the Department of Indian Affairs, 1914, Reports of Indian Agents, page 56.

[174] <u>Sessional Papers of Canada, 1916</u>, Report of the Department of Indian Affairs, 1915, Reports of Indian Agents, page 59.

[175] <u>Sessional Papers of Canada, 1917</u>, Report of the Department of Indian Affairs, 1916, Reports of Indian Agents, pages 59-60.

[176] See 19, above, They Came To Wood Mountain, page 19; Wood Mountain Uplands, page 78.

[177] Conversation with Leonard Lethbridge, Lakota Sioux elder, in 2005, at the Wood Mountain reserve. Leonard lives on the reserve. His family has a tradition of preserving the history of the Lakota Sioux in Canada. I am grateful to Bill Ogle and his son, Travis, for introducing me to Leonard Lethbridge. Travis is an expert in Lakota Sioux artifacts and he is able to make reproductions of the real thing. (Also, he lets me stay at his house when I visit Wood Mountain.)

[178] A Profile of the Wood Mountain Reserve, Saskatchewan Indian, Vol. 6, No.11, page 16, Nov., 1976. On the internet: http://collections.ic.gc.ca/indian/a76nov15.htm

[179] http://www.civilization.ca From the home page, search "Wood Mountain"; click on any biography, then click on "index" to get a complete list of biographies.

[180] See 91, above, The Stone War Club. John Okute LeCaine, Letter to R. Decook, 1/1/1947, The LeCaine Family.

[181] Kingsley M. Bray, Spotted Tail and the Treaty of 1868, Nebraska History, Spring 2002, pages 20, 27.

[182] Sessional Papers of Canada, 1911, Report of the Department of Indian Affairs, 1910, Census, pages 126-127.

[183] See 3, above, Wood Mountain Lakota, page 151.

[184] See 1, above, Ibid. See 6, above, page 203.

[185] See 19, above, Wood Mountain Uplands, page 123.

[186] The memorial rides for Big Foot and Sitting Bull reached a high point in 1990, one hundred years after the massacre. 129 riders began the ride and the number increased as they approached Wounded Knee. Conger Beasley Jr., We Are A People in This World, The Lakota Sioux and the Massacre at Wounded Knee, 1995 (University of Arkansas Press), pages 3, 8, 54. Guy Le Querrec, On The Trail To Wounded Knee, The Big Foot Memorial Ride, 2000 (The Lyons Press). V. Blackhawk Aamodt and Rachel Forte, The Ghost Riders, 2005 (Paha Sapa Filmworks), DVD, 60 minutes. On page 66 of his book, Conger Beasley Jr., writes:
" I told them a story that Alex White Plume had told me. On the second Big Foot Memorial Ride there were thirty-six participants. To make up for lost time on the third day they rode at night. An hour or two after dark, Alex noticed a host of luminous sparks dancing around the horses' hooves. Periodically he and Rocky Afraid of Hawk positioned themselves at the head of the line and counted the riders as they plodded by, to make sure that none had fallen or that no horse had bolted across the countryside. The sparks that whirled up from the horses' hooves were as dense as fireflies. The last time they did their tally the line of riders seemed to go on and on. The silhouettes of the riders at the back of the line were ragged and frowzy, indicating they were wrapped in furs and buffalo robes and that they carried staffs and lances. Alex and Rocky both counted eighty-six riders. By the time they counted the last one, the hair on the back of Alex White Plume's neck was electric with fright. Silently he and Rocky rode back to the head of the line. When they reached their camp an hour later and did another tally, there were only the original thirty-six riders."

[187] Website of Aboriginal Affairs and Northern Development Canada. They keep changing there name and making it harder to find information but it's there. Population on the reserve provided by Crystal Ogle.

[188] John Okute LeCaine, Scrapbook, Rodeo-Ranch Museum, Wood Mountain, SK.

APPENDIX A
DIVISIONS OF THE SIOUX NATION AND SOME OF THEIR CHIEFS

Western (Teton) LAKOTA DIALECT	Middle (Yankton) NAKOTA DIALECT	Eastern (Santee) DAKOTA DIALECT

1. Hunkpapa
   Sitting Bull, Four Horns
   Black Moon (H), Crow King
   Crow, Iron Dog
   *No Neck
2. Mnicoujou
   Makes Room[3], Hump
   Big Foot, *Black Moon (M)
3. Oglala
   Red Cloud, Crazy Horse
   Low Dog, *White Rabbit[5],
4. Brulé
   Spotted Tail, *Black Bull[7], *Brave Heart[8]
5. Sans Arc
   Spotted Eagle
6. Two Kettle
   Runs the Enemy
7. Blackfoot[12]
   Kill Eagle
	1. Yankton
	   Strike the Ree
	2. Yanktonai
	   Drifting Goose
		1. Mdewakanton
		   Little Crow[1]
		   Waoke[2]
		   (Weeokeah)
		2. Wahpekute
		   Red Point
		   (Inkpaduta)
		3. Wahpeton
		   Rattles Walking[4]
		   (H'damani)
		   Cloud Appears[6]
		   (Mahpiyahdinape)
		   Hupa Yakta[9]
		4. Sisseton
		   White Lodge
		   White Eagle[10]
		   Standing Buffalo[11]
		   White Cap[13]
		   Tasinawakanhdi[14]

*Stayed in Canada after Sitting Bull returned to the United States, July, 1881.

---

[1] Leader of the Dakota Sioux in the 1862 Sioux War in Minnesota.

[2] Obtained a reserve in Canada in 1877 (Reserve #59A – Oak Lake)

[3] Married Sitting Bull's older sister, Good Feather. This formed a special bond between Sitting Bull's Hunkpapas and the Mnicoujou.

[4] Obtained permission from the Ojibwa, in 1862, to live in Canada at Turtle Mountain. In 1886 the land was surveyed and recorded as Indian Reserve #60. In 1891 the government began to successfully induce the people to move to other reserves in Canada or the United States. Canada cancelled the reserve in 1909. The translation of H'damani as Rattles Walking is in The Canadian Sioux by James H. Howard, 1984 (University of Nebraska Press), page 23.

[5] White Rabbit surrendered with Crazy Horse in May, 1877. The Crazy Horse Surrender Ledger, 1994 (Neb. State Hist. Society), pg. 157. In the winter of 1892-3, he led a group that split away from Black Bull.

[6] Obtained a reserve in Canada in 1874 (Reserve #57 – Birdtail Creek).

[7] Black Bull Led some Lakota Sioux to Moose Jaw in 1883. In April, 1877, two weeks prior to the surrender of Crazy Horse, Black Bull and Brave Heart transferred from the Red Cloud agency (Oglala) to the Spotted Tail agency (Brulé). See note 5, above, The Crazy Horse Surrender Ledger, pages 153, 154.

[8] Obtained a reserve in Canada in 1910 (Reserve #160 – Wood Mountain). This is the only Lakota Sioux reserve in Canada. Regarding Black Bull and Brave Heart see note 7, above.

[9] Obtained a reserve in Canada in 1894, north of Prince Albert (Reserve #94A – Wahpeton).

[10] Obtained a reserve in Canada in 1874 (Reserve #58 – Sioux Valley, Oak River).

[11] Obtained a reserve in Canada in 1877 (Reserve #78 – Standing Buffalo).

[12] Not the Blackfoot Confederacy that has reserves in Alberta or its branch that has a reservation in Montana.

[13] Obtained a reserve in Canada in 1879 (Reserve #94 – White Cap).

[14] Bought land in Canada in 1892 at Portage La Prairie (Sioux Village). This land was given up by 1957. Some of the people went to Dakota Plains or later to Dakota Tipi. In 1945, Reserve #6A, Dakota Plains (Long Plain) was created. In 1973, Reserve #1, Dakota Tipi, was created near Portage La Prairie.

Note: Information about the Dakota Sioux reserves in Canada is from The Dakota of the Canadian Northwest by Peter Douglas Elias, 2002 (Canadian Plains Research Center, University of Regina).

APPENDIX B
OVERVIEW MAP

1 inch = 112 miles

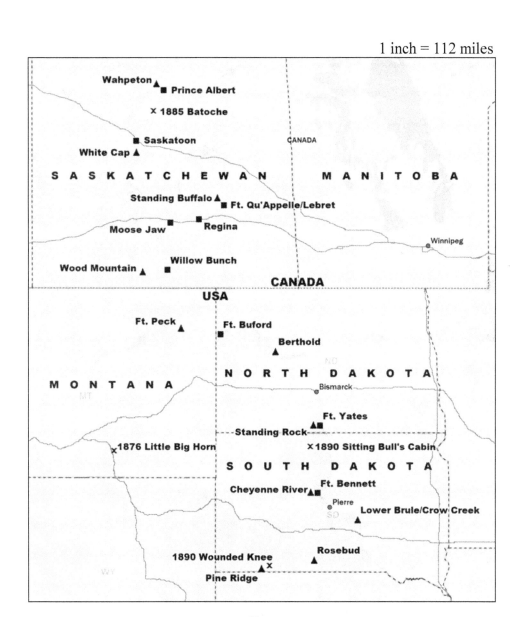

Key

▲ Indian Reserve (Canada) or Reservation (U.S.)
■ Fort, Town or City
✗ Conflict

APPENDIX C
DETAIL MAP

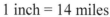

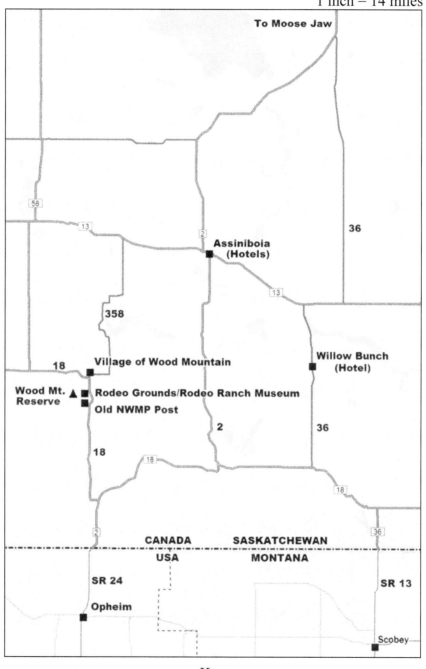

Key

▲ Indian Reserve   18   Province Road
■ Historic Site, Village or Town   SR   State Road

United States of America.
              Dr. to Jean Louis Legare.
April 20th 1881
        To Provisions, Tobacco & Pipes furnished
        Sitting Bull & followers (485) for a feast.
April 26th 1881.
        To Transportation & board furnished 16
        Indians from Woody Mountain
        N. W. T. Canada to Fort Buford D. T.
        U. S. A. distance 150 Miles @ 32 00/100 $ Each
May 4th Transportation & board for 4
        Indians from Fort Buford D. T. U. S. A.
        to Woody Mountain N. W. T. Canada.
        distance 150 Miles @ 32 00/100 $ Each.
May 23rd 1881.
        To Transportation & provisions for
        32 Indians from Woody Mountain
        N. W. T. Canada to Fort Buford D. T.
        U. S. A. @ 32 00/100 $ Each.
June 1' 1881
        To Transportation & provisions for 3
        Indians from Fort Buford D. T. U. S. A.
        to Woody Mountain N. W. T. Canada.
        @ 32 00/100 $ Each.

THE MONUMENT IN THE BATOCHE CEMETERY

CREE, Dakota Sioux, Lakota Sioux and Saulteaux (Ojibwa) took part in the Métis Resistance of 1885 in the Batoche area.[1] A monument in the Batoche Cemetery lists the names of Métis and Indians who died in the three engagements that took place in the Batoche area (Duck Lake, Fish Creek and Batoche). Four Indian names are listed. A reference binder in the Batoche Visitor Center gives the battle where each Indian died. The names of the Indians and where they died are:

AH-SI-WE-IN	(Duck Lake)
WAH-PI-TI-WA-KI-PE	(Fish Creek)
CHA-PI-TO-LA-TA	(Fish Creek)
JA-PA-TO-PA	(Batoche)

It is said that some of these names may be Lakota Sioux.[2] The first name is a Cree.[3] The second name is "Joli Corbeau" (Pretty Crow), the son of Little Crow (not the famous chief), who was Dakota Sioux.[4] The third name includes an "L" sound. It is probably Lakota Sioux because the "L" sound is common in their dialect but is absent from the dialects of the other tribes present at the battles.[5] We also know that this Indian was killed instantly.[6] I speculate this is "Tormenting Bear" (Mato Wakaesija).[7] The fourth name may be the son, or adopted son, of Chief White Cap, who was Dakota Sioux.[8] Some Nakota Sioux were part of Chief White Cap's band, so their dialect is also a possibility when interpreting these names.[9] Another possibility is that the names are in Michif, the Métis language that combines French and Plains Cree.

In 1888 the Métis military leader, Gabriel Dumont, said two Sioux were killed at Fish Creek and two Sioux were killed at Batoche (not counting a 12 year old Sioux girl killed at Batoche).[10] If Dumont is correct, there is at least one Sioux Indian missing from the monument. Red Bear (Mato Luta) was a Lakota Sioux who was put on trial for his part in the Métis resistance of 1885. He died from his battle wound or from sickness, while serving his prison sentence.[11] If Dumont knew of Red Bear's death, that is the name missing from the monument; if not, there are at least two Sioux Indian warriors missing from the monument.

APPENDIX E-2
ENDNOTES

[1] Gabriel Dumont, translated by G.F.G. Stanley, <u>Dumont's Account of the North West Rebellion</u>, The Canadian Historical Review, XXX, Sept. 3, 1949, page 259.

[2] Gontran Laviolette, <u>The Dakota Sioux in Canada</u>, (DLM Publications, 1991), page 253. Thelma Poirier, Ed., <u>Wood Mountain Uplands from the Big Muddy to the Frenchman River</u>, 2000, (Wood Mountain Historical Society, Box 53, Wood Mountain, Saskatchewan S0H 4L0, Canada), page 72. Bonnie Day and Thelma Poirier, <u>Wood Mountain Lakota</u>, 1997, (Saskatchewan Heritage Foundation, 1919 Saskatchewan Drive, 9th Floor, Regina, Saskatchewan S4P 4H2, Canada, phone: (306)787-4188), page 37.

[3] Blair Stonechild and Bill Waiser, <u>Loyal Till Death, Indians and the North-West Rebellion</u>, (Fifth House LTD, 1997), pages 65-69.

[4] Ibid., page 156. See 2, above, <u>The Dakota Sioux in Canada</u>, page 253.

[5] Email from Professor Mary C. Marino, Ph.D., Department of Languages Linguistics, University of Saskatchewan, 9 Campus Drive, Saskatoon, Canada S7N 5A5.

[6] See 3, above, page 156 and note 28 citing <u>Compte rendu de l'abbe G. Cloutier</u>, 1886, vol. 1, 2-9.

[7] See 2, above, <u>Wood Mountain Uplands</u>, pages 72-73; <u>Wood Mountain Lakota</u>, page 37.

[8] See 3, above, pages 152 and 163. Bob Beal and Rod Macleod, <u>Prairie Fire, The 1885 North-West Rebellion</u>, (McClelland & Stewart Inc, 1994), pages 161 and 229. General Sir Fred Middleton, <u>Suppression of the Rebellion in the North West Territories of Canada</u>, 1885, Edited, with Introduction, By G. H. Needler, (University of Toronto Press, 1948), pages 26-27.

[9] See 2, above, <u>The Dakota Sioux in Canada</u>, page 252. Gontran Laviolette, <u>The Sioux Indians In Canada</u>, (Marion Press, 1944), page 118.

[10] See 1 above, pages 262 and 266. See 3, above, <u>Loyal Till Death</u>, page 163.

[11] See 2, above, <u>Wood Mountain Uplands</u>, pages 72-73; <u>Wood Mountain Lakota</u>, page 37. Leonard Lethbridge, a great grandson of Red Bear, lives on the Wood Mountain reserve. He says Red Bear may have died from sickness, such as pneumonia, due to poor prison conditions.

APPENDIX F
PHOTOGRAPH OF INDIAN NAMES
ON THE BATOCHE MONUMENT

(Photograph by Ron Papandrea, Summer, 2001)

"A Sioux took care of the rifles at Batoche. He was very good at it."

Gabriel Dumont[1]
Military Leader of the Métis in 1885

"Uncle, when one wants to go and rescue his friends,
he does not wait for the next day."

Yellow Blanket[2]
Spoken to Gabriel Dumont at Fish Creek

"The Great Spirit denied me a grave in the Battlefield;
I have to die a poor natural death."

Chief Brave Heart[3]
Wood Mountain Lakota Sioux

---

[1] Gabriel Dumont, translated by Michael Barnholden, <u>Gabriel Dumont Speaks,</u>
1993 (Talonbooks), page 28.

[2] Bob Beal & Rod Macleod, <u>Prairie Fire, The 1885 North-West Rebellion</u>, 1994
(McClelland & Stewart Inc.), pages 231-232.

[3] John Okute Le Caine, <u>The Stone War Club</u>, Moose Jaw Public Library Archives,
Sioux Indians.

THE TRIAL OF TWO LAKOTA SIOUX

ON September 17, 1885, five Indians, including two Lakota Sioux, were put on trial in Regina for their part in the Métis Resistance of 1885. There are two sources that must be examined: The trial report[1] and the list of cases in the North-West Territories for 1885.[2] A problem arises in attempting to understand these sources because four of the five Indians are identified by one name in the trial report and a different name in the list of cases. The list of cases is needed because it gives sentencing information that is missing from the trial report. In the trial report, the Indians are numbered (1-5) and their names are:

1)The Hole   2)Red Eagle 3)Poor Crow 4)Red Bean 5)Left Hand

The list of cases names the same five Indians:

1)White Dog 2)Red Eagle   3)Little Crow 4)Red Bear   5)The Lame Man

Red Bean/Red Bear was a Lakota Sioux with "Red Bear" being the correct name.[3] Poor Crow/Little Crow was a Lakota Sioux with "Poor Crow" being the correct name.[4] Red Eagle, correctly identified in both sources, was the son-in-law of Chief White Cap and a member of his band (Chief White Cap was a Dakota Sioux).[5] The Hole/White Dog was a Dakota Sioux.[6] Left Hand/The Lame Man was a Cree.[7]

All five Indians were tried together and a jury found them guilty of "treason-felony". Four of the five were sentenced to three years imprisonment; Red Eagle was sentenced to six months,[8] possibly in deference to his relationship to Chief White Cap. The sentences of three years were reduced to one year, due to the effort of Father Albert Lacombe on behalf of all Indian prisoners.[9]

Red Bear died from his battle wound while serving his prison sentence.[10] The descendants of Red Bear live on today in the Lethbridge family.[11] Poor Crow served his sentence and joined the Lakota Sioux at Moose Jaw. He is also known as Lean Crow.[12] The descendants of Poor Crow can be found today in the Goodtrack family.[13]

APPENDIX G-2
ENDNOTES

1   QUEEN VS. OKA-DOKA ET AL., Sessional Papers of Canada, 1886, No. 52.

2   Settlers and Rebels, 1882-1885, The Official Reports of the North-West Mounted Police, Facsimile Edition, (Coles Publishing Company, 1973), Appendix O for 1885.

3   Thelma Poirier, Ed., Wood Mountain Uplands from the Big Muddy to the Frenchman River, 2000, (Wood Mountain Historical Society, Box 53, Wood Mountain, SK S0H 4L0, Canada), pages 72-73. Bonnie Day and Thelma Poirier, Wood Mountain Lakota, (Saskatchewan Heritage Foundation, 1919 Saskatchewan Drive, 9th Floor, Regina, Saskatchewan S4P 4H2, Canada, phone: (306)787-4188), pages 35-37.

4   Kirk Goodtrack, Wood Mountain Lakota Sioux Legal Submission, Claims to Compensation for Lands 1870 Imperial Order in Council, June 14, 2004, submitted to the Department of Indian Affairs, page 173, reprinting Thomas Aspdin, List of the Teton Sioux at Present at Moose Jaw and Vicinity, October 28, 1896, PAC RG 10 Vol. 3599 File 1564 B.

5   See 1, above, QUEEN VS. OKA-DOKA ET AL., testimony of John W. Astley.

6   See 1, above, QUEEN VS. OKA-DOKA ET AL. The Hole's Indian name was Oka Doka. The "D" indicates a Dakota name. Hs was not the Cree because Left Hand was identified as the Cree.

7   See 1, above, QUEEN VS. OKA-DOKA ET AL.

8   See 2, above, Settlers and Rebels, Appendix O for 1885.

9   See 3, above, Wood Mountain Lakota, page 37.

10 See 3, above, Wood Mountain Lakota, page 37; Wood Mountain Uplands, page 73.

11 See 3, above, Wood Mountain Lakota, page 35; Wood Mountain Uplands, page 72.

12 See 3, above, Wood Mountain Lakota, page 37; Wood Mountain Uplands, page 73.

13 http://www.civilization.ca From the home page, search "Wood Mountain"; click on any biography; then click on "index; then click on "Ayuta Najin Ktewin (Killed the Enemy That Stood Looking / Susan Goodtrack).

APPENDIX H
POSSIBLE PHOTOGRAPH OF BLACK BULL & WIFE
(They would be sitting on the right)

FRANK YATES · SHORT BULL · LONE BULL · CHARLES B. GORDON ("DEADWOOD CHARLIE") · FEATHERS ON-HIS-HEAD · FIRE THUNDER · MRS. FEATHERS ON-HIS-HEAD

There are two versions of this photograph with different captioning. The version discussed on page 13 of the main text, referenced in endnote 58, labels the woman "Mrs. Black Bull Bear" and the Indian sitting on the far left "Black Bull Bear". The version above is from the Denver Public Library. "Frank Yates" and "Deadwood Charlie" are clues to the place and time of the photograph. Frank Yates was the brother of Captain George Yates, killed with Custer. Frank was a trader at Spotted Tail and Red Cloud agencies, 1874-1877. In January, 1876, he ran a stage line via these agencies to the Black Hills. He left the area in 1878. The Black Bull who led the "Moose Jaw Sioux" was a Brulé Lakota who could have been at Spotted Tail agency prior to June, 1876. The photograph could have been taken at Spotted Tail or Red Cloud agencies. Deadwood was founded in the summer of 1875; no one would be called "Deadwood Charlie" until that time. Black Bull was at the Little Big Horn, June 25, 1876. Allowing time for his travel, the photograph could have been taken Summer, 1875 to May, 1876. Tom Buecker, Red Cloud Agency Traders, 1873-1877, The Museum of the Fur Trade Quarterly, Vol 30, No. 3, Fall, 1994, pages 6-12. Agnes Wright Spring, The Cheyenne and Black Hills Stage and Express Routes, 1948 (University of Nebraska Press), pages 81-83. (Photograph courtesy of the Denver Public Library, X-33524)

APPENDIX I
GRAVE OF TASINASKAWIN
(Mrs. Black Bull)

(Photograph by Ron Papandrea, Summer, 2003)

APPENDIX J
GRANDDAUGHTERS OF BLACK MOON
(The Mnicoujou Chief)

Left to right: Emma Loves War and Okute Sica (LeCaine Family)
He Killed Two (Big Joe) and Katrine Loves War (Ferguson Family)

Thanks to Wood Mountain Post Provincial Park.

APPENDIX K-1
LETTER OF HAYTER REED

Office of the Indian Commissioner
Regina, August 28th, 1890

To: The Deputy of the
Supt. Gen'l of Indian Affairs,
Ottawa

Sirs:

With reference to your letter No. 85892 of the 26th June last, and prior correspondence respecting the Sioux Indians residing in the neighborhood of Moose Jaw, I have the honor to inform you that these Indians were twice visited by the Assistant Commissioner, since the receipt of your letter, namely on (July 22nd) and (August 6th). In order to secure a better result from the interview, Mr. (James) Thompson (Thomson), the Sioux Interpreter of the Mounted Police at Wood Mountain, was kindly authorized by the Commissioner of Police to come to Moose Jaw for the purpose of acting as Interpreter at the first visit. Unfortunately, however, only three heads of families turned up at the meeting, the others having scattered in various parts of the country South of Moose Jaw.

In accordance with your instructions the Indians present were informed of the desire of the Department that they should remove with the balance of the Band to their own reservations across the line. They were shown that their squatting on land not their own in the midst of a growing settlement, was not only a cause of annoyance to settlers, but a source of great hardship to themselves. From the point of view of their own welfare and future of their children they were strongly urged to go back to their respective reservations where they had a right to be and share in the many advantages connected therewith. It was the desire of the Department that they should all leave willingly and peacefully, but in case of refusal on their part, every legal means would be resorted to, in order to secure their removal from the country.

The three Indians present engaged to repeat to the others, at the first opportunity, what they themselves had been told. Mr. Thompson, the Interpreter was also requested to make it known to all those he might meet on his way back to Wood Mountain. Mr. Thomas W. Aspdin, a resident of Moose Jaw, who possesses a fair knowledge of the Sioux language and who lives in the immediate vicinity of the Indian Camps, engaged also to keep the subject before them, and to inform this office of their movements.

APPENDIX K-2

On (August 4th), Mr. Aspdin wrote that Rising Bear, one of the three Indians seen by the Assistant Commissioner, was showing a determination to leave, but was in need of some assistance to supply himself and family for the journey. There being a hope that the departure of Rising Bear would be the signal for others to follow, I instructed the Assistant Commissioner to proceed again to Moose Jaw with authority to tender all reasonable help which, under the circumstances, he might judge advisable.

This second visit of my Assistant was made on (August 6th), and I have now much pleasure to inform you that "Rising Bear", "Seechah"[1], and "The Lungs"[2] left for the Standing Rock Agency on (August 13th) with three lodges of Indians. Two more lodges were expected to leave with them, but backed out at the last moment.

Mr. Aspdin who appears to be unremitting in his efforts, in his letter informing me of the departure of the above named Indians, states that one of the lodges that backed out, did so, on account of the action of some white people in Town, who wished them to stop as they employ them around their houses. He adds that the Indians supply a cheap labor and most of the Townspeople will be sorry to see them go. No doubt this is the key to the whole difficulty. The Indians would long since have left, had it not been for the influence exercised by persons interested to retain them. More efforts will however be made and it is to be hoped that they will result in these Sioux gradually leaving the country.

The expense incurred for the assistance given to the three lodges that have left, amount to $15.40, which will, I trust, meet with your approval.

I have the honor to be,
Sir,
Your obedient servant,

Hayter Reed
Commissioner

---

[1] Seechah (The Thigh) was associated with the Burnt Thigh (Brulé) and Oglala branches of Lakota Sioux. This is Brave Heart, who later became the Chief of the Wood Mountain Lakota Sioux. John Okute LeCaine, The Stone War Club, Moose Jaw Public Library Archives, Sioux Indians. They Came To Wood Mountain, 4th Edition, 1995 (Wood Mountain Historical Society), page 19.

[2] The Lungs belonged to the "Two Kettle" branch of the Lakota Sioux. He is mentioned in: E.H. Allison, Surrender of Sitting Bull, 1892, reprinted in South Dakota Historical Collections, Vol. VI, 1912, pages 238-239.

UNITED STATES INDIAN SERVICE,
Office of Indian Agent,
Cheyenne River Agency, S.D.
August 5, 1891.

Thomas W. Aspdin,
Moose Jaw, Assiniboia,
North-West Territory, Canada.

Sir:

I am in receipt of a communication from the Hon. Commissioner of Indian Affairs, inclosing copy of letter sent to this office dated January 2nd, 1891, inquiring as to the whereabouts of an Indian named Black Moon; also inclosing letter addressed to the Commissioner of Indian Affairs relating to the same subject matter.

For your information relative to the family of Black Moon, I would respectfully state that Black Moon and family arrived at this agency about November 1st. 1890, coming from the Standing Rock Agency, and were taken up on the rolls, and given a ration ticket. The names as recorded on census book (*for 1891) are as follows:

Black Moon	Male	70 yrs.
Two Lance	Male	25
--------Red Lodge	Female	47
Jumps or Skip	Male (sic)	23
Many Arrows (*Philip)	Male	12 yrs.
Touching Killed	Male	14
Spotted Horse	Male (sic)	4

This family is now living on this reservation about 70 miles from the agency; the two boys aged 12 and 14 respectively were sent to the "boys boarding School" and will return to the school at the beginning of the school year.

Since receiving the letters referred to I have sent for Black Moon and learn from him that another family, relatives of his, came with him from Canada but did not report at this agency (*meaning they did not go to Fort Bennett during the Ghost Dance "Outbreak") but remained in Big Foot's camp and went with him to Pine Ridge Agency: there was four members of this family, three of which were killed at the Wounded Knee affray, the remaining one being wounded and still at the Pine Ridge Agency. The names of the family were as follows:

White Dog, son of Black Moon, Killed
Yellow Ear, daughter of Black Moon, Killed
Rattling Wind, wife of Black Moon, Killed

High Back (*son of Black Moon), wounded. As this family did not report at the agency (*during the Ghost Dance "outbreak") but were in the company of other Indians from the Standing Rock Agency (*refugees from the Sitting Bull killing) they were known as Standing Rock Indians.

Black Moon wishes me to say to you that he intends to remain here: he likes the people here because they are all peaceable and satisfied; he is living with his son Two Spear who has a good home; he is not far from an issue station; he thinks you could come and see him; he wants you to know that he has been well treated here (*despite having three family members killed and one wounded) and that he will send the two boys to the boarding school. Trusting that this information may be satisfactory, I am, sir,

Very respectfully,

Perain P. Palmer
U.S. Indian Agent

*Remarks added by Ron Papandrea

APPENDIX M
ORDER IN COUNCIL NO. 1775

AT THE GOVERNMENT HOUSE AT OTTAWA
Tuesday, the 5th day of August, 1930

PRESENT

HIS EXCELLENCY THE GOVERNOR
GENERAL IN COUNCIL

HIS Excellency the Governor General in Council, on the recommendation of the Right Honorable the Prime Minister, for the Minister of the Interior, and under and by virtue of Section 74, chapter 113, R. S. 1927, is pleased to order that the lands as described hereunder be and they are hereby withdrawn from the operation of the said Act and set apart for the use of the Indians as Wood Mountain Indian Reserve No. 160.

Description:

Being in the fourth township, in the fourth range, west of the third meridian, in the Province of Saskatchewan, and composed of the northeast quarter of section thirteen, the whole of sections twenty-two, twenty-three, twenty-four, twenty-five, thirty-four, thirty-five and thirty-six, the northeast quarter of section twenty-six and the northwest quarter and south half of section twenty-seven, all of the said township, as the said sections and parts of sections are shown upon a map or plan of survey of the said township, approved and confirmed at Ottawa, on the 3rd day of September, A.D. 1910, by Edouard Deville, Surveyor General of Dominion Lands, and of record in the Department of the Interior; the lands herein described containing by admeasurement together five thousand two hundred and eighty acres, more or less.

E. J. LEMAIRE,
Clerk of the Privy Council

Source: Canada Gazette, Vol. 64, July-September, 1930, page 509.

APPENDIX N
MAP OF WOOD MOUNTAIN INDIAN RESERVE NO. 160
(9.25 Sq. Miles - 5,920 Acres)

WOOD MOUNTAIN

WOOD

MOUNTAIN

INDIAN RESERVE

NO. 160

FROM J. LECAINE

FROM HBC

FROM HBC   FROM HBC

|___1 Mile___|

Sources:
Map of <u>Rural Municipality of Waverley No. 44</u>, Revised May, 1999,
Rural Municipality Office, Glentworth, Saskatchewan S0H 1V0.
Map of <u>Rural Municipality of Old Post No. 43</u>, Revised April, 1999,
Rural Municipality Office, Wood Mountain, Saskatchewan S0H 4L0.

APPENDIX O-1
LAKOTA SIOUX AT MOOSE JAW AND WOOD MOUNTAIN

Year	Date	Notes	Moose Jaw Population	Lakota at Moose Jaw In Winter/In Summer				Lakota at Wood Mountain In Summer (*on reserve)			Lakota Total	Lakota Living On Reserve		
				In Winter	M	F	T	M	F	T		M	F	T
1881	7-19		Sitting Bull returns to the U.S. - In Canada there remain over 200											
1884	1-18	A	720											
1885	June	B,C	800				80							
1885	8-24	D					48							
1887	1-18	B,E	800	100										
1889	6-11	F									150			
1890		B	900											
1892	12-30	G		115										
1893		B	1,200											
1894		B	1,500											
1896	10-28	H					80			11				
1900	9-06	I									125			
1901	3-31	D	1,558				88							
1901	8-02	I									125			
1902	8-04	I									120			
1903	6-30	I									110			
1903	11-20	J	3,200											
1904	8-15	I									112			
1905	6-30	I									119			
1906	6-30	D	6,249				110							
1907	3-31	I									112			
1908	3-31	I									115			
1909	3-31	I									117			
1910	3-31	I									121			
1910	July	K								92				
1910	10-29		Lakota Sioux obtain a temporary reserve at Wood Mountain.											
1911	3-31	I									124			
1911	6-01	D	13,823		21	22	43							
1912	3-31	I									124			
1912	10-25	L								130*				
1912 & 1913		M	Last Camps at Moose Jaw.											
1913	3-31	I									124			
1914	3-31	I									124			
1916	3-31	I									124			
1916	6-01	D	16,934		1	0	1							
1917	3-31	I									124			51
1921	6-01	D,N	19,285		0	1	1	55	48	103*				
1924	3-31	I												40
1926	6-01	D	19,039					49	47	96*				
1929	3-31	I												42
1930	8-05		Lakota Sioux reserve at Wood Mountain is made permanent.											

APPENDIX O-2
LAKOTA SIOUX AT MOOSE JAW AND WOOD MOUNTAIN

Year	Date	Notes	Moose Jaw Population	Lakota at Moose Jaw In Winter/In Summer			Lakota at Wood Mountain In Summer (*on reserve)			Lakota Total	Lakota Living On Reserve		
				M	F	T	M	F	T		M	F	T
1931	6-01	D	21,299								19	18	37
1936	6-01	D	19,805								21	27	48
1941	6-02	D	20,753								23	14	37
1946	6-01	D	23,069								23	19	42
1951	6-01	D	24,355								30	25	55
1956	6-01	D	29,603								21	19	40
1961	6-01	D	33,206								16	14	30
1966	6-01	D	33,417								23	14	37
1971	6-01	D,O	31,850								25	10	35
1976	6-01	D	32,581								20	10	30
1981	6-03	D	33,941								5	5	10
1986	6-03	D	35,073										16
1991	6-04	D	33,593										8
1996	5-14	D	32,973										18
2001	5-15	D	32,131										**10
2002	6-01	P								***199	8	4	12
2003	6-01	P								***205	8	4	12
2004	5-01	P								***208	8	4	12
2005	5-01	P								***214	8	4	12
2006	5-16	D											17
2006	6-01	P								***216	6	4	10
2007	6-01	P								***218	6	4	10
2011	5-10	D											**15
2012	12-01	P								***270	4	4	8

**Results under 15 are rounded to the nearest 5.
***These figures show registered band members only.
Other people may live on the reserve.

APPENDIX O-3
1896 LIST OF LAKOTA SIOUX AT MOOSE JAW AND VICINITY
by Thomas Aspdin (Note H)

Indian Name	English Name	Location 10/28/1896	No. In Family	Remarks
1. Chatah	The Hawk	Wood Mountain	4	*Note M.
2. Chatcah	Left Handed	Moose Jaw	3	
3. Pootay	The Upper Lip	Moose Jaw	7	aka Joe
4. OKootay	The Shooting Man	Moose Jaw	6	
5. No genny wanitch	No Ears, Deaf Man	Wood Mountain	2	
6. Ista Sappa	Black Eyes	Wood Mountain	5	
7. Ta Tonka Sappa	Black Bull	Old Wives Creek	2	aka Bruly, *Lame Brulé
8. Nitaylah	The Rump	Moose Jaw	6	
9. Eh-you-kay-lah	The Antlers	Moose Jaw	3	
10. Wambilee	The Eagle	Moose Jaw	3	His wife is a Cree Women
11. Shumgah-non-e-Sappa	Wild Black Horse	Moose Jaw	3	
12. Mary and Her Mother		Moose Jaw	2	*Mary Black Moon, wife of Aspdin
13. Ochesley	Dung	Moose Jaw	6	aka Bokas
14. Jack Bruley's widow & Family		Moose Jaw	3	
15. Seechah	The Thigh	Moose Jaw	4	*aka Brave Heart, Burnt Thigh, Si & Cy (Note Q)
16. Mush-in-sih	*Jack Rabbit	Moose Jaw	4	aka Bogue, & *Teal Duck (Note R)
17. Congee-tam-aichih	Poor Crow	Moose Jaw	4	*Lean Crow
18. Tah-Shungah-free	Shooting at the Horse	Moose Jaw	4	
19. Pay-zootah-wichen	Medicine Man	Moose Jaw	2	
20. Nupayways	Bloody Hand's family	Moose Jaw	7	
21. Shungah-hoska	Long Dog (Note S)	Moose Jaw	2	aka Crazy Jack
22. Mushin scah	White Rabbit	Moose Jaw	2	aka Big Jim (Note T)
23. Ta-shun-machtag	Good Robe	Moose Jaw	2	
24. Antelope's widow & FamilyMoose Jaw			5	Known as Aunty, her son is Long Chicken
		Total	91	and 1 family at Regina and 1 family at Qu'Appelle

*Added by Ron Papandrea

APPENDIX O-4
NOTES

A. Population of Moose Jaw when it incorporated as a town. <u>Population of Moose Jaw 1883-1998</u>, Moose Jaw Public Library Archives, referring to the <u>Moose Jaw News</u>, January 18, 1884.

B. Moose Jaw Population: Ibid., referring to <u>Henderson Directory</u>.

C. Lakota Sioux Population: Leith Knight, <u>all the moose…all the jaw</u>, 1982 (Moose Jaw 100), page 11, letter of Private O'Donnell.

D. Canadian Census Data.

E. Lakota Sioux Population: Bonnie Day and Thelma Poirier, <u>Wood Mountain Lakota</u>, 1997 (Saskatchewan Heritage Foundation, 1919 Saskatchewan Drive, 9th Floor, Regina, Saskatchewan S4P 4H2, Canada, phone: 306-787-4188), page 41, referring to John Taylor, Report to the Indian Commissioner, Jan. 18, 1887, RG-10, Vol. 3652, File 8589, Pt. 2.

F. <u>Assistant Adjutant Gen., Division of the Missouri, to Adjutant Gen., U.S. Army</u>, June 11, 1889, McLaughlin Papers, roll 33, State Historical Society of North Dakota, Bismarck, N.D.

G. <u>Sessional Papers of Canada, 1893</u>, Report of the North-West Mounted Police, 1892, Appendix D, page 50.

H. Kirk Goodtrack, <u>Wood Mountain Lakota Sioux Legal Submission, Claims to Compensation for Lands 1870 Imperial Order in Council</u>, June 14, 2004, submitted to the Department of Indian Affairs, page 173, reprinting Thomas Aspdin, List of the Teton Sioux at Present at Moose Jaw and Vicinity, October 28, 1896, PAC RG 10 Vol. 3599 File 1564 B. I have included Black Bull and his wife in the Moose Jaw total, although they were at Old Wives Creek at the time.

I. <u>Sessional Papers of Canada</u>, Report of the Department of Indian Affairs, Indian Census and/or Indian Agent Report for the year stated. The Lakota Sioux report is part of the report for the Assiniboine Agency (Reserve #76), Carry-the-kettle; and the "Moose Jaw Sioux" are sometimes listed in the Indian Census under the Assiniboine Agency, Carry-the-kettle.

J. Population of Moose Jaw when it became a city. <u>Moose Jaw Times-Herald</u>, June, 25, 1953, Jubilee Supplement, page 30.

K. See E, above, page 59, referring to Graham, RG-10, Vol. 7779, File 27137-1.

L. <u>Sessional Papers of Canada, 1913</u>, Report of the Royal Northwest Mounted Police,1912, Appendix K, page 165.

M. The last recorded Lakota Sioux camps at Moose Jaw where in 1912 and 1913. In the winter of 1912-13, there was a camp of five lodges: two belonged to Big Joe (He killed Two), one to Old Man Hawk, one to Yellow Hawk and one to Julia Lethbridge (the daughter of Red Bear, who died in prison following the Métis Resistance of 1885). Julia had 8 children, 5 boys and 3 girls. Indians Of Moose Jaw, Big Joe, information supplied by George LeCaine, nephew of Big Joe, January 17th, 1969. They Came To Wood Mountain, 4th Edition, 1995, page 249. In the summer of 1913 there was a Lakota Sioux camp at Moose Jaw. The Moose Jaw Evening Times, September 13, 1913, Remnants of Sioux Indians Who Camp Near Moose Jaw, page 6.

N. From 1921-1976, each Canadian Census lists the Lakota Sioux under Saskatchewan Census Division #3, Indian Reserves (the Lakota Sioux have the only reserve in this census division). For the 1981 census, and each census thereafter, the Lakota Sioux are listed under Saskatchewan Census Division #3, Wood Mountain 160.

O. An error in the census table reports only five females at the Wood Mountain Reserve.

P. Website of Aboriginal Affairs and Northern Development Canada. They keep changing their name and making it harder to find information but it's there. Figures include registered band members only. Other people may live on the reserve.

Q. See M, above, The Moose Jaw Evening Times, page 6 and They Came To Wood Mountain, page 19. Brave Heart became a chief of the Wood Mountain Lakota Sioux.

R. See M, above, The Moose Jaw Evening Times, page 6, photograph of Bogue, named after an early Moose Jaw settler, Richard Bogue; and Gontran Laviolette, The Dakota Sioux in Canada, 1991 (DLM Publications), photograph of Teal Duck. The photographs are the same.

S. This is not the famous chief with the same name.

T. White Rabbit became a chief when the band at Moose Jaw split into two groups in the winter of 1892-3. He is buried in Weyburn, Saskatchewan. Burial information is from M, above, They Came To Wood Mountain, page 249.

CANADIAN DEPARTMENT OF INDIAN AFFAIRS – STATISTICS

The statistics on the following pages are mostly for Lakota Sioux living on the Wood Mountain Indian Reserve. They are mainly compiled from the annual reports of the Department of Indian Affairs published in the Sessional Papers of Canada.

Table 1A - Census – Religion

Date	Anglican	Presbyterian	Roman Catholic	Other Christian	Native Belief	Total
6-30-1902		3	1		116	120
6-30-1903		3	1		106	110
3-31-1910		6	4		111	121
3-31-1917					51	51*
3-31-1924	5		9	5	21	40*
3-31-1929			42			42*

Table 1B – Census - Population Detail

Date	Under 6		6–15		16–20		21–65		65 & Up		Births	Deaths	Total
	M	F	M	F	M	F	M	F	M	F			
3-31-1910	11	11	12	11	7	7	28	29	3	2	5	1	121
3-31-1924	1	4	2	1	2	1	15	8	1	5	**	**	40*
3-31-1929	2	4	0	5	0	1	13	9	3	5	**	**	42*

*Living on the Wood Mountain Indian Reserve.
**Not recorded.

Table 2 - Grain, Vegetable and Root Production

Year Ending	Wheat		Oats		Other Grains		Peas, Beans, etc.		Potatoes		Other Roots		Wild Hay
	Acres	Bushels	Acres	Bushels	Acres	Bushels	Acres	Bushels	Acres	Bushels	Acres	Bushels	Tons
3-31-1917			10	500	1	20			8	240			150
3-31-1918			20						3	325	1	25	230
3-31-1919			10				3	8	5.5	135	2.5	17	260
3-31-1924	74	*	99	500	47	507			3	185			117
3-31-1925	45	860	35	**	72	851			2	115			114
3-31-1926	14	280			75	1,000			3	125			200
3-31-1927	80	1,200	30	1,500	101	700			6	200			110
3-31-1928	84	390	40		50	***			1	25			77
3-31-1929	84	390	40		50				1	25			77
3-31-1930	84	275							1	25			75

*   Hailed out.
**   Cut for feed.
*** Cut green – Rust.

Table 3A - Land: Buildings and Real Property

Date or Year Ending	Acres of Reserve*	Acres of Wood	Acres Cleared but not Cultivated	Acres Under Cultivation	Acres Fenced	Stone, Brick & Frame Dwellings	Other Dwellings (Pole & Adobe)	Out-Buildings, etc.	Council Houses (Public Property)
10-29-1910	10,240	Temporary reserve was created.							
6-30-1911	10,240	Sessional Papers of Canada 1912, 21A, Handbook of Indians of Canada, pg. 521.							
3-31-1917	11,520	5	11,485	30	640	0	15	15	0
3-31-1918	10,240	5	10,200	35	640	0	15	14	1
3-31-1919	11,520	10	11,487	23	1,280	0	11	15**	0
3-31-1924	5,280	200	4,857	223	800	0	12	14	0
3-31-1925	5,280	256	4,857	167	800	0	13	15	1
3-31-1927	6,720	1,160	5,200	360	800	0	14	16	1
3-31-1928	6,720	190	6,270	260	800	0	13	15	1
3-31-1929	6,720	190	6,270	260	800	0	13	15	1
3-31-1930	6,720	190	6,370	160	800	0	13	15	1
8-05-1930	5,280	Permanent reserve was created.							
10-07-1930	5,760	Three quarter-sections of Hudson's Bay land were added to the reserve.							
1954	5,920	The quarter-section of John LeCaine was added to the reserve.							

* See next page, The Changing Size of the Reserve.
**An error in the table indicates "5".

APPENDIX P-4
THE CHANGING SIZE OF THE RESERVE

The Canadian west is surveyed using the township system. Each township is six miles by six miles. Each square mile (section) is divided into quarters (quarter-sections). Each quarter-section is 160 acres. A township is said to be so many townships north of the U.S. border and so many townships west (its range) of a surveyed demarcation line, called a meridian. The 1st meridian was near Winnipeg; the 2nd meridian was about 200 miles west; the 3rd meridian was about another 180 miles west. The township containing the Lakota Sioux reserve was the 4th township north of the U.S. border and the 4th township west of the 3rd meridian; abbreviated: 4-4 W3.

The early reports on the size of the reserve vary between 10,240 acres and 11,520 acres. Originally, the reserve occupied the entire north half of the township minus one quarter-section. One quarter-section in the south half of the Township was added to balance off the missing quarter-section in the north; so the total size of the reserve was ½ of a township, which is 72 quarter-sections (11,520 acres). However, eight quarter-sections within the reserve were legally set aside for other uses: four quarter-sections in the western half of the reserve were set aside for school use (could be sold to finance schools); three quarter-sections in the eastern half of the reserve were owned by the Hudson's Bay Company; one quarter-section in the eastern half of the reserve was homesteaded and owned by John LeCaine. Subtracting these eight quarter-sections from the reserve made its legal size 10,240 acres and thus we can explain the varying reports on the size of the reserve, depending on whether you include quarter-sections legally set aside for other uses. (See map, P-5.)

World War I ended in 1918 and the western half of the reserve was opened for settlement by veterans. The size of the reserve (not including the three quarter-sections of Hudson's Bay land and the one quarter-section owned by John LeCaine) was reduced to 5,280 acres. The quarter-section in the southern half of the township was kept in the reserve to give this total. Charles LeCaine, the brother of John LeCaine and a World War I veteran, obtained a quarter-section by soldier settlement. His soldier settlement land was next to the reserve but in the township to the east. This acreage is not included in any of these calculations.

In the Indian Affairs reports for 1927 through 1930, the size of the reserve was 6,720 acres; an addition of nine quarter-sections. I speculate the additional land may have been unclaimed or lost soldier settlement land that reverted to the reserve; or, it may have been land transferred to the reserve as a source of wood and agricultural production (notice the increase in acres of wood and agricultural production for 1927). Whatever the reason for the increase, this land was not included as part of the permanent reserve.

On August 5, 1930, the reserve was made permanent at a size of 5,280 acres. On October 7, 1930, the three quarter-sections owned by the Hudson's Bay Company were transferred to the reserve, bringing it up to 5,760 acres. In 1954, John LeCaine transferred his quarter-section to the reserve, making it 5,920 acres. (See map, P-6.)

APPENDIX P-5
MAP OF TEMPORARY RESERVE – OCTOBER 29, 1910

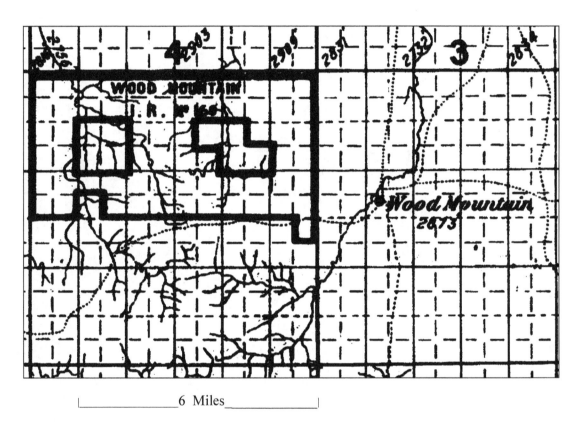

|_____6 Miles_____|

Source: Wood Mountain, Sectional Sheet No. 18, 1st February, 1916, NMC 0084501.

APPENDIX P-6
MAP OF PERMANENT RESERVE – AUGUST 5, 1930

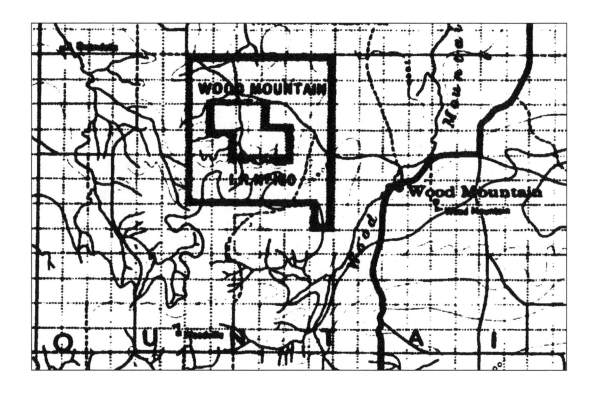

Source: Wood Mountain, Sectional Sheet No.18, April, 1930, NMC 0084502.

Table 3B - Personal Property

Year Ending	Ploughs, Harrows, Drills, etc.	Mowers, Reapers, Binders, Threshers, etc.	Carts, Wagons & Vehicles	Automobiles	Tools & Smaller Implements
3-31-1917	2	8	18		200
3-31-1918	2	4	34		250
3-31-1919	6	4	30		81
3-31-1924	11	11	18		82*
3-31-1925	11	9	18		82
3-31-1926	11	9	18		90
3-31-1927	12	11	19	1	90
3-31-1928	10	14	20	1	140
3-31-1929	10	14	20	1	140
3-31-1930	10	14	20	1	140

* An error in the table indicates "28".

APPENDIX P-8

Table 4A - Live Stock and Poultry

	Horses			Cattle					Poultry
Year Ending	Stallions	Geldings & Mares	Foals	Bulls	Steers & Work Oxen	Milk Cows	Young Stock	Other Stock	
3-31-1917		82	33		4				34
3-31-1918	2	80	10		4				35
3-31-1919	2	103	22		3	1			.....
3-31-1924	1	95	11	1	4	2	8	5	131
3-31-1925	2	130	40		16	7	8	6	160
3-31-1926	2	100	45			6		25	150
3-31-1927	1	74	16			1	1		253
3-31-1928		107	1	1	2	4			25
3-31-1929		107	1	1	2	4			25
3-31-1930		73			2	4			25

Table 4B - General Effects

Year Ending	Rifles & Shot Guns	Steel Traps	Tents
3-31-1917	9	36	13
3-31-1918	10	40	15
3-31-1919	13	42	13
3-31-1924	1	33	7
3-31-1925	16	20	13
3-31-1926	16	20	12
3-31-1927	14	24	15
3-31-1928	13		13
3-31-1929	13		13
3-31-1930	13		13

Table 5A - Value of Real Property

Year Ending	Total Value of Lands in Reserve	Value of Private Fencing	Value of Private Buildings	Value of Public, Buildings, Property of the Band
	C$	C$	C$	C$
3-31-1917	57,600	150	1,200	
3-31-1918	51,200	150	1,150	
3-31-1919	57,600	500	1,200	
3-31-1924	15,840	25	1,945	
3-31-1925	15,840	25	1,200	100
3-31-1926	15,840	25	1,200	100
3-31-1927	10,400	100	1,400	100
3-31-1928	15,840	20	1,000	100
3-31-1929	15,840	20	1,000	100
3-31-1930	15,840	20	1,000	100

Table 5B – Value of Personal Property

Year Ending	Value of Implements & Vehicles	Value of Live Stock & Poultry	Value of General Effects	Value of Household Effects	Total Value of Real & Personal Property
	C$	C$	C$	C$	C$
3-31-1917	1,000	5,560	2,150	1,000	68,660
3-31-1918	1,295	5,600	1,500	1,250	62,145
3-31-1919	1,700	4,120	500	2,100	67,720
3-31-1924	800	2,740	462	930	22,747
3-31-1925	1,200	4,100	300	850	23,615
3-31-1926	1,200	3,600	350	875	23,190
3-31-1927	1,500	4,650	400	900	19,450
3-31-1928	1,500	4,000	300	800	23,560
3-31-1929	1,500	4,000	300	800	23,560
3-31-1930	1,000	2,500	300	800	21,560

Table 5C - Value of Improvements

Year Ending	Value of New Land Improvements	Value of Buildings Erected	Total Increase in Value
	C$	C$	C$
3-31-1917	75	150	225
3-31-1918	100	75	175
3-31-1919	250		250
3-31-1924			
3-31-1925	300		300
3-31-1926			
3-31-1927	400	200	600
3-31-1928			
3-31-1929			
3-31-1930			

Table 6 - Sources and Value of Income

Year Ending	Value of Farm Products, Including Hay	Value of Beef Sold Also of That Used for Food	Wages Earned	Received From Land Rentals & From Timber	Earned by Hunting & Trapping	Earned by Other Industries & Occupations	Annuities Paid, & Interest on Indian Trust Funds	Total Income of Indians
	C$	C$	C$	C$	C$	C$	C$	C$
3-31-1917	1,390.00		857.00	50.00	100.00	55.00		2,452.00
3-31-1918	1,550.00		350.00	150.00	150.00	900.00		3,100.00
3-31-1919	1,712.00		2,020.00	100.00	50.00	150.00	6,296.24	10,328.24
3-31-1920							6,296.24	6,296.24
3-31-1921							6,500.00	6,500.00
3-31-1924	1,321.00	884.00	150.00		50.00			2,405.00
3-31-1925	3,000.00	2,700.00	500.00				2.88	6,202.88
3-31-1926	3,200.00	2,800.00	600.00		400.00		1.88	7,001.88
3-31-1927	3,900.00	1,200.00	500.00		300.00		1.88	5,901.88
3-31-1928	1,239.00	125.00	875.00		80.00		2.07	2,321.07
3-31-1929	1,239.00	125.00	875.00		80.00		2.18	2,321.18
3-31-1930	1,125.00		875.00		80.00		2.29	2,082.29

APPENDIX Q
SOME POPULATIONS ON THE NORTHERN PLAINS

CANADIAN PLAINS

Cities, Towns & Villages		Indian Reserves		
Calgary, AB	878,866	Standing Buffalo	443*	DAKOTA: Sisseton, Wahpeton
Edmonton, AB	666,104			Total Membership: 1,211*
Winnipeg, MB	619,544	White Cap	283*	DAKOTA: Sisseton
Saskatoon, SK	196,811			Total Membership: 600*
Regina, SK	178,225	Wood Mountain	8*	LAKOTA: Mixed Group
Moose Jaw, SK	32,131			Total Membership: 270*
Assiniboia, SK	2,483			
Lebret	2,207			
Fort Qu'Appelle	1,940			
Willow Bunch	395			
Limerick	146			
Wood Mountain	40			

NORTHERN U.S. PLAINS

Cities		Indian Reservations		
Minneapolis, MN	382,618	Fort Peck	10,321	DAKOTA: Sisseton, Wahpeton,
St. Paul, MN	287,151			Wahpekute
Sioux Falls, SD	123,975			NAKOTA: Yanktonai, Assiniboine[1]
Fargo, ND	90,599			LAKOTA: Hunkpapa
Billings, MT	89,847	Cheyenne River	8,470	LAKOTA: Mnicoujou, Two Kettle
Rapid City, SD	59,607			Sans Arc, Blackfoot
Bismarck, ND	55,532	Standing Rock	8,250	LAKOTA: Hunkpapa, Blackfoot
Minot, ND	36,567			NAKOTA: Yanktonai
Butte, MT	33,892	Pine Ridge	15,521	LAKOTA: Oglala, Brulé
Mandan, ND	17,225	Rosebud	10,469	LAKOTA: Brulé, Oglala
Williston, ND	12,512	Lower Brulé	1,362	LAKOTA: Brulé
Hardin, MT	3,384	Crow Creek	2,225	NAKOTA: Yanktonai

Sources:
2001 Canadian Census
2000 United States Census
Michael Johnson, <u>The Tribes Of The Sioux Nation</u>, (Osprey, 2000), page 9.

*As of December 1, 2012. Website of Aboriginal Affairs and Northern Development Canada. They keep changing their name and making it harder to find information but it's there. These figures show registered band members only. Other people may live on the reserve.

---

[1] The Assiniboine separated from the Sioux Nation prior to 1600 but retained their Sioux dialect (Nakota).

INDEX

Little Big Horn Battlefield, June, 2003
(Photograph by Ron Papandrea)

The Author

Ron Papandrea was born November 9, 1948, of Italian-American parents, Sam and Elizabeth (Gandini) Papandrea. He earned a Bachelor of Science degree from the College of Social Science at Michigan State University and a Juris Doctor degree from Wayne State University Law School. Ron is a life member of the Custer Battlefield Historical & Museum Association. His haiku poetry has been published in *Stroker* magazine. He lives in Warren, Michigan, but likes to roam.

ronpapandrea@gmail.com

TheyNeverSurrendered.com

The seven campfires shall return.

The seven campfires shall return.

With this prayer,

The seven campfires shall return.

CPSIA information can be obtained
at www.ICGtesting.com
Printed in the USA
LVHW100959301219
642058LV00013B/139/P

9 780974 652771